UNIVERSITY STRATEGY 2020

"This report will be of great value to university leaders and their advisers. At times it will be uncomfortable reading because it has a ruthless focus on what is important in good strategy. It shines a light on the weaknesses and strengths of existing university strategies and will hopefully help the next tranche of missions, values, visions, performance indicators and the like all line up to much greater effect."
>Lord Jim Knight, Chief Education and External Officer, TES Global Ltd

"This is a very interesting and insightful report, especially for those of us in the sector whose roles are about helping our universities to shape their future."
>Dr Richard Hutchins, Director of Strategy, University of Warwick

"The need for a UK university to have a purposeful strategy which is comprehensible to its staff, students, and other stakeholders has never been greater. Mike Baxter provides an evidence-based framework that will enable institutions to develop a strategy that is clear and accessible, and consequently will help them to achieve their ambitions."
>Dr Mark Skippen, Head of Marketing Intelligence, Swansea University

"Given the maelstrom universities are currently working within, this modern, up-to-date guidance around strategy development is timely. The insights are delivered in straightforward and clear language."
>John Britton, Head of Planning and Intelligence, Cardiff University

"Mike's report is a thorough and detailed survey of HEI strategies; it is insightful in many ways and a very useful reference for anyone engaged in strategy development and implementation."
>Steve Chadwick, Director of Strategy, Planning and Change, University of Bristol

"This report provides a unique overview of strategic plans in the UK higher education sector, highlighting good practice and common pitfalls. The proposed Strategy Design Framework should be a useful tool for universities, guiding the sector towards a more mature approach to strategy development"
>Dr Hulda Sveinsdottir, Director of Planning, University of Aberdeen

University Strategy 2020:
Analysis and benchmarking of the strategies of UK Universities

Dr Mike Baxter
Goal Atlas Ltd

UNIVERSITY STRATEGY 2020

Copyright © 2019 Mike Baxter

All rights reserved.

CONTENTS

	Executive Summary	i
	About this report	iii
	About the Author	iv
	Acknowledgements	iv
1	Making Sense of Strategy	1
	~ The Language and Structure of Strategy	1
	~ The Hallmarks of Good Strategy	3
	~ Elements of Strategy	5
	~ How Strategy Works	8
2	University Strategies: Overview	9
	~ Vision, Mission and Values	12
3	Strategy Element: Destination	19
4	Strategy Element: Methods	23
5	Strategy Element: Alignment	26
6	Strategy Element: Innovation	34
7	Strategy Element: Priority	39
8	Strategy Element: Performance	42
9	Strategy Element: Agility	46
10	Strategy Element: Adoption	52
11	University Strategies: The Future	57
12	Key Recommendations	60
	Appendix 1	65
	References	70

CONTENTS

	Executive Summary	i
	About this report	iii
	About the Author	iv
	Acknowledgements	iv
1	Making Sense of Strategy	1
	~ The Language and Structure of Strategy	1
	~ The Hallmarks of Good Strategy	3
	~ Elements of Strategy	5
	~ How Strategy Works	8
2	University Strategies: Overview	9
	~ Vision, Mission and Values	12
3	Strategy Element: Destination	19
4	Strategy Element: Methods	23
5	Strategy Element: Alignment	26
6	Strategy Element: Innovation	34
7	Strategy Element: Priority	39
8	Strategy Element: Performance	42
9	Strategy Element: Agility	46
10	Strategy Element: Adoption	52
11	University Strategies: The Future	57
12	Key Recommendations	60
	Appendix 1	65
	References	70

EXECUTIVE SUMMARY

This report aims to help senior leaders and those involved in shaping the strategic direction of universities to make sense of strategy. We do this by firstly exploring the current landscape of strategy in the university sector based on analysis of 52 published UK university strategies and 28 one-to-one interviews with senior individuals in the sector. Our research examines the language and structure of strategy presented in strategy documents, and identifies four hallmarks of good strategy – challenge, choice, coherence and change. The research analyses universities' statements of their vision, mission and values, and identifies three different types of aspirations in vision statements: university status/reputation, social impact and student impact. We propose a model that shows how strategy serves to combine mission, vision and values, namely that strategy is the plan of action that connects mission to vision, based on an organisation's values and current state, and responsive to both opportunities and obstacles.

Based on our sample of 52 UK university strategies:
- 69% refer to their strategy document as either a 'Strategy' or a 'Strategic Plan'. Other 'labels' included Corporate Strategy, Strategic Framework and Corporate Plan.
- 54% have KPIs; 14% have targets (i.e. values used as a threshold to define success) associated with KPIs.
- 58% had at least an in-depth summary of their strategy available on their website. 19% had an introductory video. 85% had a downloadable .pdf.
- 52% covered a 5-year time period. The range was between 3 and 20 years, although 13% did not specify a time frame.
- The median word count was 3,267; the longest was 11,225.
- The median number of pages was 16 and the longest was 77.

- 71% included a vision statement, 62% included a mission statement and 65% included a statement of their values. 35% had all three and 8% had none.
- 73% had status- or reputation-based aspirations in their vision statements. 51% had social-impact aspirations. 49% had student-impact aspirations.
- 46% had statements of values (rather than narrative). Of these, the most frequently used words related to inclusion, excellence, ambition, integrity, innovation, professionalism, respect, collaboration, community, creativity, diversity, fairness and sustainability.

The report examines in detail, chapter by chapter, eight elements of strategy that form a framework for good strategy design, based on best-practice strategic thinking from the commercial sector. Key recommendations for the university sector are identified for each element of this Strategy Design Framework as summarised below:

Strategy Element	Description	Summary of key recommendations
Destination	Where we are striving to get to	Define a coherent and meaningful purpose that is clear, focused, people-oriented and based on a need to change. Employ vision and values to provide stability and continuity across strategies.
Methods	Core activities to reach our destination	Identify a handful of pivotal core methods that are both sufficient and necessary to achieve strategic success (i.e. to get to the strategy destination).
Alignment	The logic connecting actions to outcomes	Ensure strategy is actionable across internal and external operating environments, and meets the need to change. Ensure internal consistency between strategies and sub-strategies.
Innovation	The cultivation of new ways of thinking and working	Define innovation in terms of how it will drive change - what innovation is needed, why it is needed and how it will be both pursued and measured. Recognise and plan for resources, disruption and risks involved. Avoid 'fluff'.
Priority	The identification of what really matters	Clearly identify, justify and set priority levels to ensure timely and effective allocation and deployment of resources.
Performance	Data indicative of meaningful progress	Commit to measuring performance to assess strategic impact, and define that performance measurement process. Ensure consistent use of measurement (e.g. KPIs and targets). Include performance-based contingency plans.
Agility	The ability and readiness to change	Ensure key parts of strategy are fit to respond swiftly and appropriately to foreseeable and unforeseeable challenges and opportunities. Be vigilant, then refresh and re-prioritise in a strategic, customer-centric and evidence-based way.
Adoption	Active engagement, willing commitment	Be explicit about how strategy is to be adopted. Consult during strategy development and promote strategy launch. Ensure strategically-aligned resourcing and rigorous strategy governance and management.

Figure i Summary of key recommendations for university strategy development

The report concludes by looking towards the future for university strategies. With the sector facing huge challenges (marketplace competition, changes in financial models and increasingly demanding 'customers'), and with 62.5% of the strategies analysed ending by 2021, this is a critical time for strategic thinking in the university sector. University strategies will need to have more 'bite', more impact, and become increasingly honest and transparent about the challenges they face, and increasingly focused about how they intend to respond.

ABOUT THIS REPORT

The stimulus for this research came from strategic work that the author, Dr Mike Baxter, has been undertaking in the commercial sector for over fifteen years. This work has led to the development of a design framework for strategy: what are the key purposes a strategy should serve in large, complex 21st century organisations, and what components should a good strategy contain to serve those purposes well? The research behind this report was intended to test, refine and elaborate this Strategy Design Framework.

So, why UK universities, and why now? UK universities present great opportunities for strategy research:
- They are a big global success. The UK has 1% of the world's population and 9% of the top 1,000 global universities.
- They form a large, commercially important sector of the UK economy.
- The sector faces huge challenges; marketplace competition, changes in financial models and increasingly demanding 'customers'. It therefore needs powerful, effective strategies to respond to those challenges.
- Universities publish their strategies; no commercial or industrial sector is strategically so open.

The research for this report was conducted between December 2018 and February 2019 and had two sources. The first source was an in-depth analysis of the published strategies of 52 UK universities. These universities were selected using 4 criteria:
1. a selection of Russell Group and non-Russell Group universities;
2. high-ranking universities and those that had the biggest recent changes to their university rankings (up or down);
3. representations of universities from across the UK, including some that were in geographically similar locations (for comparison purposes)
4. a selection of small specialist universities.

The universities selected for this research are listed in Appendix 1.

The second source was a series of 28 one-to-one interviews (phone or face-to-face, typically 45 minute duration) with senior individuals with responsibility for, or influence over, university strategy. These included a former Government Minister, Vice Chancellors, senior managers with direct responsibility for writing or managing university strategy (with titles including Pro-Vice-Chancellor or Director of Strategy) and providers of strategic services to the university sector.

About the Author

Dr Mike Baxter is former Professor and Dean of Ravensbourne University and was Director of the Design Research Centre at Brunel University. Since 2001, Mike has been an independent researcher, author and business consultant. Most of his recent work has been focused on the digital transformation of large global brands (Cisco, Google, Skype, Sony PlayStation, HSBC and Roche are all former clients).

Mike's company, Goal Atlas Ltd, was founded in 2014 to develop tools, processes and software for strategy design and adoption. Goal Atlas provides a full range of support services for all stages of strategy development from preparation and production to implementation, measurement and governance. www.goalatlas.com.

Acknowledgements

We would like to thank all those who took part in the interviews for this research, including the following:

- Professor Robert Allison, Vice-Chancellor and President, Loughborough University
- Matt Atkin, Director of Planning, University of Manchester
- Anna Barber, Director of Strategy, The Open University
- Helen Barton, Director of Strategic Planning, Manchester Metropolitan University
- John Britton, Head of Planning and Intelligence, Cardiff University
- Liz Bromley, Joint Interim Institutional Lead and Deputy Vice-Chancellor (Corporate Planning and International Strategy), University of Central Lancashire
- Professor David Cardwell, Pro-Vice-Chancellor (Strategy and Planning), University of Cambridge
- Steve Chadwick, Director of Strategy, Planning and Change, University of Bristol
- Paul Colbran, Chief Information and Infrastructure Officer, Solent University
- Professor Chris Day, Vice-Chancellor and President, Newcastle University
- Mike Deyes, Deputy Director of Marketing (Digital), University of Liverpool
- Martyn Edwards, Associate Director (Marketing, Intelligence, and Digital), Swansea University

- Kelly Harrison, Head of Online Services, University of the Arts London
- Dr Richard Hutchins, Director of Strategy, University of Warwick
- Simon Jennings, Director of Strategic Planning and Governance, Lancaster University
- Professor Andy Kent, Pro-Vice-Chancellor for Strategic Planning, Kingston University London
- Lord Jim Knight, Chief Education and External Officer, TES Global Ltd
- Dr Lynne Livesey, Joint Interim Institutional Lead and Deputy Vice-Chancellor (Academic), University of Central Lancashire
- Fiona Loughran, Director of Planning, University of Portsmouth
- Professor Nick Petford, Vice-Chancellor, University of Northampton
- Wesley Rennison, Director of Strategic Planning, University of Dundee
- Ester Ruskuc, Director of Strategy and Policy, University of St Andrews
- Dr Mark Skippen, Head of Marketing Intelligence, Swansea University
- Dr Hulda Sveinsdottir, Director of Planning, University of Aberdeen
- Steve Walsh, Head of Planning, Aberystwyth University

1 MAKING SENSE OF STRATEGY

Higher education has been through some turbulent changes over the past decade. Revenue sources for universities have diversified significantly[1] and competition for students has intensified[2].

These changes have been described as "increasing marketization and instability of the HE environment"[3] requiring "root and branch changes in governance".[4]

Universities have responded strategically. Moran and Powell suggest that "a more strategic approach was seen as key to success in the sector".[5] According to Sir David Bell, Vice Chancellor of the University of Sunderland[6] "the rise of strategy" has been one of the big themes, as seen through the eyes of vice chancellors over the past ten years.

Whilst strategy may have been recognised by universities as important, this doesn't necessarily mean their strategies have been successful. Sir David Bell is concerned that "for all the effort that went into seeking distinctiveness, [university] strategy documents ended up looking remarkably similar."

We will explore this issue of distinctiveness in some detail in Chapter 3 of this report, but before we do so we need to be clear about what strategy is, and what it is comprised of.

The Language and Structure of Strategy

This report is based on an analysis of 52 strategy documents published by UK universities. To be meaningful, this needs to be built around a common understanding of the language used to label parts of strategy and the logical relationships between those labelled parts.

Let's start with the organisation in its current state – the baseline for any strategy. Many organisations commit significant time and resources to auditing and analysing their current state.

That current state is determined to a large extent by the organisation's mission. The word 'mission' literally means a specific task with which a person or a group is charged[7] or a strongly felt aim, ambition, or calling.[8] An organisation's mission is a statement of core purpose and focus that normally remains unchanged over time.[9] It answers the question, "Why does our business exist?"[10]. A mission statement communicates the organisation's purpose to its employees, customers, suppliers and other stakeholders and creates a sense of identity for its employees.[11]

Then the organisation's vision is set out. This is almost a counter-point to its current state (Figure 1). It defines where we are not currently, but want to be. The word 'vision' literally means the act or power of seeing or imagining,[12] or the ability to think about or plan the future with imagination or wisdom.[13] An organisation's vision is a picture of its potential;[14] it depicts what the organisation will look like in the future.[15] A good vision statement should be short, simple, specific to your business, leave nothing open to interpretation, and should have ambition.[16] It should be an audacious dream of a future reality based on the work you do.[17] It should inform, inspire and energise everyone in the organisation.[18]

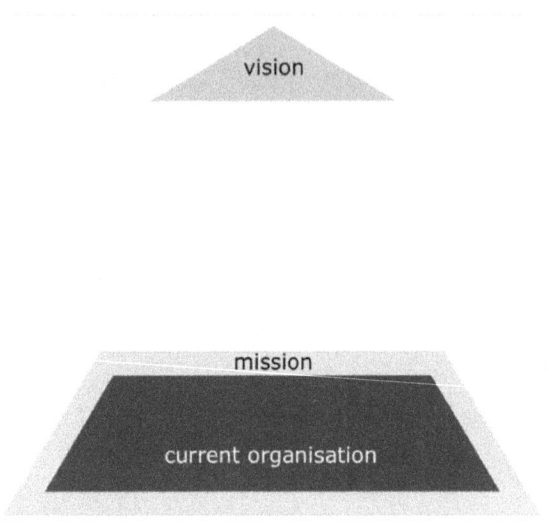

Figure 1 Vision is a counterpoint to an organisation's current state

Strategy is how we move from where we are now towards where we want to be. It is what connects current state with vision (Figure 2). A strategy is "a plan of action designed to achieve a long-term or overall aim".[19] It is a plan of action, not a dream, not a vision, not an aspiration and not a hope. A strategy is also designed to achieve an aim. It is about change. It is about achieving something that would not otherwise come about if a plan of action hadn't been successfully executed. Richard Rumelt, author of 'Good Strategy Bad Strategy', one of the best-selling strategy books of recent years, says strategy must "identify the critical obstacles to forward progress and then develop a coherent plan to overcome them".[20] Failing to recognise that there are critical obstacles facing the organisation is one of Rumelt's indicators of bad strategy. A strategy is also specific. It is a plan to undertake a coordinated set of

Figure 2 Strategy is the plan of action that connects mission to vision, based on an organisation's values and current state, and responsive to both opportunities and obstacles.

actions, over a stated timescale to overcome identified obstacles or exploit recognised opportunities and hence achieve an overall aim.

Strategy is driven by, and constrained by the organisation's values. The word 'values' literally means principles or standards of behaviour; one's judgement of what is important in life;[21] the moral principles and beliefs or accepted standards of a person or social group.[22] Values are the ethical ideals of the organisation.[23] They are important and lasting beliefs or ideals shared by the members of a culture about what is good or bad and desirable or undesirable.[24]

The Hallmarks of Good Strategy

There are four key factors that transform 'thoughts-about-the-future' into a strategy: these are challenge, choice, coherence and change. We call these the hallmarks of good strategy (Figure 3).

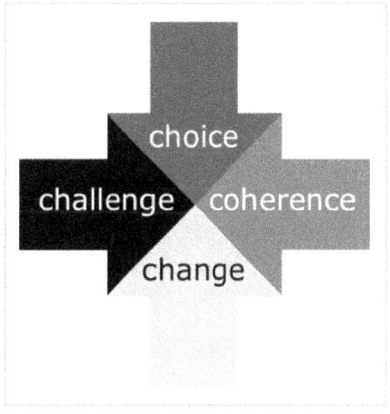

Figure 3 The Hallmarks of Good Strategy

1. **Strategy is about challenge**. Rumelt is emphatic about the importance of identifying the challenges underlying strategy. "A good strategy does more than urge us forward toward a goal or vision. A good strategy honestly acknowledges the challenges being faced and provides an approach to overcoming them."[25] "Bad strategy may actively avoid analyzing obstacles because a leader believes that negative thoughts get in the way."[26] "Strategic challenges [are the factors exerting] a decisive influence on an organisation's likelihood of future success."[27] The main strategic challenges to consider are external to the organisation. What changes are happening in the marketplace, to customers, competitors and suppliers? What political, economic, social and technological changes are foreseeable? In an environment that is volatile, ambiguous, complex and uncertain (VUCA factors),[28] scenario planning can form a critical role in identifying challenges and their likely impact on the organisation[29].

2. **Strategy is about choice**. Michael Porter, claimed to be the founder of modern strategy thinking, has championed the fact that strategy is mostly about choice. "The essence of strategy is choosing to perform activities differently than rivals do."[30] Clearly, the closer you get to considering all plausible options, the more likely you are to choose the best. This requires insightful diagnosis. As Rumelt describes it "A great deal of strategy work is trying to figure out what is going on. Not just deciding what to do but the more fundamental problem of comprehending the situation."[31] AG Lafley, former CEO of Proctor and Gamble says "In my now forty-plus years in

business, I have found that most leaders do not like to make choices. They'd rather keep their options open. Choices force their hands, pin them down, and generate an uncomfortable degree of personal risk … in effect, by thinking about options instead of choices and failing to define winning robustly, these leaders choose to play but not to win."[32] When it comes to the mechanics of making strategic choices, Rumelt's advice is to look for the levers of competitive advantage. He gives the example of Stephanie, a local shop owner trying to fend off competition from a nearby supermarket. She had a multitude of choices available to her including staff changes (regular friendly staff who'd get to know the locals), stock changes (fresh organic produce or discounted Asian products for the local student population) and a variety of discounts and promotions. It was only when she decided to focus on 'serving the busy professional who has little time to cook' that her choices became simpler and more obvious. Rumelt describes this as a 'guiding policy' – an "overall approach for overcoming the obstacles highlighted by the diagnosis".[33]

3. **Strategy is about coherence**. According to Roger Martin, currently ranked the world's leading management thinker,[34] "Strategy is … one integrated set of choices: what is our winning aspiration; where will we play; how will we win; what capabilities need to be in place; and what management systems must be instituted?"[35] Rumelt suggests "Unlike a stand-alone decision or a goal, a strategy is a coherent set of analyses, concepts, policies, arguments, and actions that respond to a high-stakes challenge."[36] He goes on to say "To have punch, actions should coordinate and build upon one another, focusing organizational energy."[37] Achieving coherence is difficult, especially across different parts of the organisation. Donald Sull, from the MIT Sloan School of Management, asked managers how frequently they could count on others to deliver on their promises. 84% said they could depend on their own manager and line reports all or most of the time but this figure dropped to 59% when it ran to individuals in other functions or departments within the organisation.[38]

4. **Strategy is about change**. This is almost a truism, but simply assuming it rather than examining it can make strategy a lot harder to develop and deploy. By being clear that strategy is about change, we can focus attention on aspects of the organisation that actually need to change. The strategy doesn't need to cover everything that we do. If catering or student accommodation or digital infrastructure or the Library are critical to achieving the changes we seek to bring about, they need to be included in the strategy. If not, leave them out. This, in turn, focuses attention on how much change is sought within a strategy. Change is disruptive, expensive, hard work and often stressful to those making it happen. It should be sought sparingly and only ever for good reasons. Clearly, for an organisation in desperate circumstances, massive change may be critical for survival. Most of the university leaders we talked to for this report, however, saw a bright future for their organisation with only modest change

needed to get there. They could continue to invest the majority of their resources into continuing to do what they already did well, leaving only a minority of resources available to drive change. Their strategies, therefore, need to reflect the amount of change they are willing to invest in.

So, a well-designed strategy is "a plan of action designed to achieve a long-term or overall aim"[39] that defines:

- what we intend to change;
- over what time period;
- by what means.

By contrast, a badly designed strategy is:

- a projection of how the world, or a market, or a business will be at some time in the future;
- a statement of future achievement without a reasoned proposal on how to get there;
- a declaration of the current strengths of an organisation and how these will continue to succeed without the need for change;
- a detailed execution plan for who is doing what, by when, with which resources and with what intended outcome.

Elements of Strategy

In the most general terms, a well-designed strategy can be thought of as comprising three layered elements. What we intend to change can be thought of as the destination we will strive to reach over the time period of the strategy. Destination derives from identity. Who we seek to be that is not simply the same as everyone else. It is why students will want to study here, why staff will want to work here, why the local community will care about us. It can be values-driven. It can be vision-led. It can be to do with place or specialisms or culture. It can be about being first or being best. Or, as will be the case with most organisations, it will be about having a distinctive blend of several different qualities. But it must be sufficiently distinctive to matter. An organisation that strives to be good at

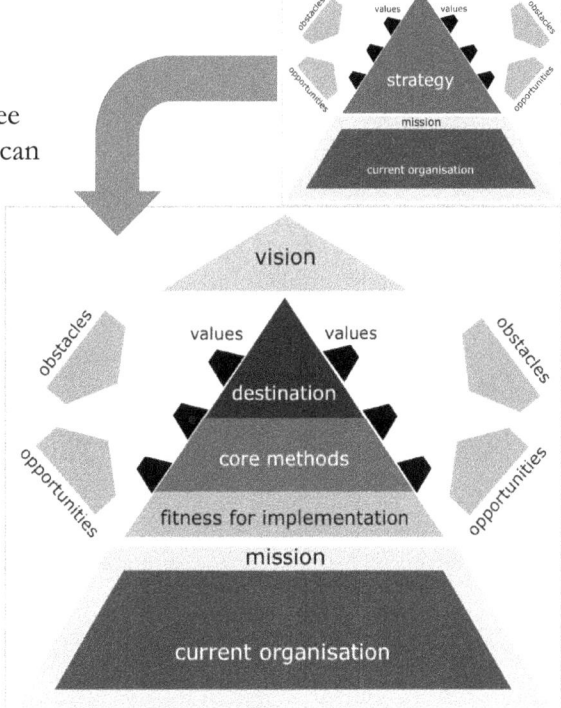

Figure 4 Elements of Strategy

everything will be out-performed and perhaps ultimately replaced by other organisations that decide to be good at something and focus their efforts and resources to achieve it. Richard Rumelt refers to this as the inherent advantage in merely having a strategy. "The first natural advantage of good strategy arises because other organizations often don't have one ... instead they have multiple goals and initiatives that symbolize progress, but no coherent approach to accomplish progress other than 'spend more and try harder'."[40]

In order to reach that destination we need to focus our efforts on the few things that will make a big difference. The coming-together of a small number of ambitious endeavours that, in combination, will bring about the transformative change most strategies seek. These are our 'Core Methods'.

And then finally we need to make sure that our strategy is fit for implementation. A strategy is not the same as an implementation plan but it does need to be fit for implementation, i.e. it needs to be well-aligned, prioritised and readily adopted across the organisation. Ideally it will cultivate new ways of thinking and working, and be responsive to performance results and external challenges and opportunities.

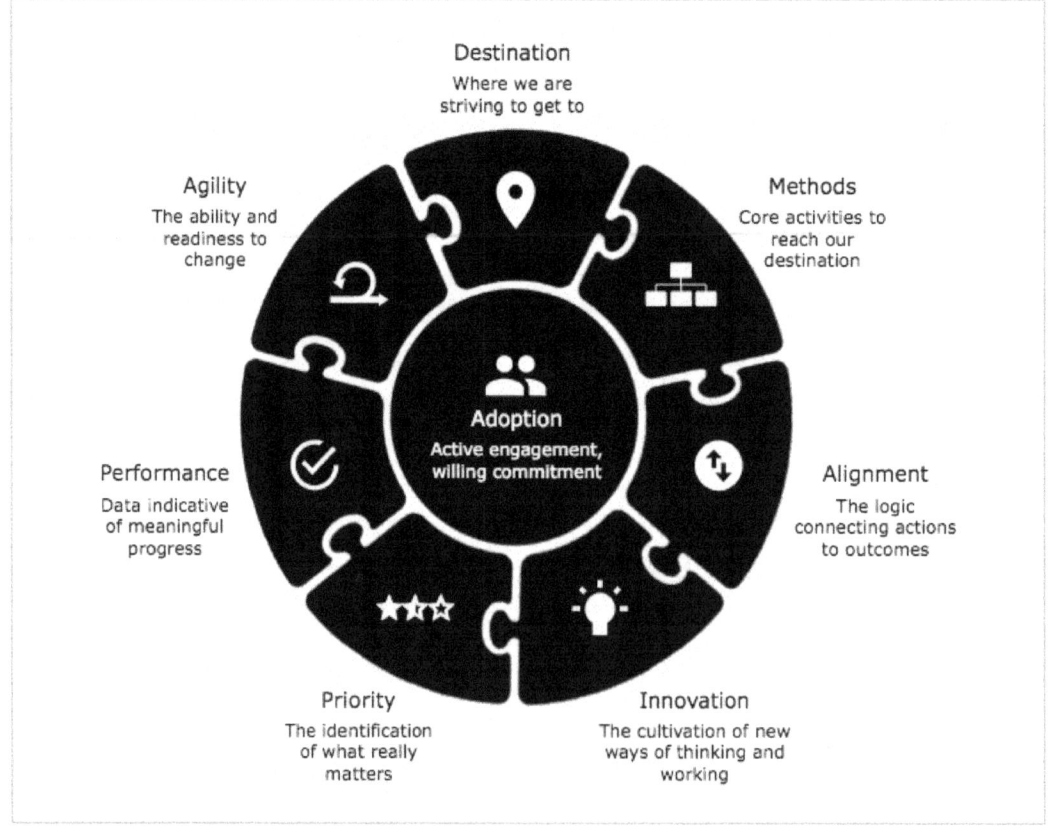

Figure 5 Strategy Design Framework

By exploring strategy design in greater detail in this way, a much richer mix of design elements starts to emerge than our simple three-layer model (Figure 4) can cope with. This more detailed view of strategy design reveals eight tightly interlinked elements that every good strategy should contain. These eight elements make up what we call a Strategy Design Framework (Figure 5), and are each explored in detail in Chapters 3 to 10.

The eight elements are as follows:
1. Destination – where we are striving to get to.
2. Methods – core activities to reach our destination.
3. Alignment – the logic connecting actions to outcomes. This is probably the biggest, the hardest and the most important challenge in strategy design. Remember the importance of coherence. If everyone in your organisation is pulling in the same direction, you will achieve more and achieve it quicker than if they are pulling in different directions.
4. Innovation – the cultivation of new ways of thinking and working. Some changes will take root within an organisation simply by being asked for (or demanded). Most, however, will not. They will require a commitment of effort, possibly by many people and probably with dedicated resources. They will require risks to be taken and failure to be tolerated. The innovation needed and how it will be supported should be specified as part of strategy design.
5. Priority – the identification of what really matters. Peter Drucker, known as the 'founder of modern management'[41] says "No business can do everything. Even if it has the money, it will never have enough good people. It has to set priorities. The worst thing is to do a little bit of everything. It is better to pick the wrong priority than none at all."[42]
6. Performance – data indicative of meaningful progress. "What gets measured, gets managed!"[43] Whilst this may be true, it is not always a good thing if the changes that matter most are the hardest to measure (e.g. aspects of culture change within an organisation). The measurement of progress serves two purposes: firstly, it justifies continued commitment to the strategy and secondly it informs course-correction and fine-tuning of strategy implementation.
7. Agility – the ability and readiness to change. According to Rita Gunther McGrath, author of the best-selling 'The End of Competitive Advantage'[44] "the traditional approach of building a business around a competitive advantage and then hunkering down to defend it … no longer makes sense."[45] "Instead, organizations need to forge a new path to winning: capturing opportunities fast, exploiting them decisively, and moving on even before they are exhausted."[46] A key element of strategy is defining how the organisation is going to respond to change, how it is going to move fast and take advantage of new opportunities as they arise.
8. Adoption – active engagement, willing commitment. The success of every strategy depends on the support it can recruit from the individuals needed to bring about change. Often this is described as strategy deployment but we have called it adoption:

less push, more pull. Putting people at the centre of strategy design ensures their involvement, commitment and active engagement. The governing body and senior leadership need to adopt the strategy and ensure their decisions both support the strategy and avoid eroding or undermining it. Front-line employees and key stakeholders (students, suppliers, business partners etc.) need to think and work in ways conducive to making the changes sought by the strategy. Middle managers are, according to Behnam Tabrizi, a Stanford Professor and best-selling author on organisational transformation, the most critical for strategy adoption. His research[47] showed that the involvement of managers two or more levels lower than the CEO was a critical factor in the success of transformative initiatives. Lack of such involvement leads to the 'frozen middle' and the demise of strategic change.

The identification of these elements is vital for analysing and benchmarking existing strategies – the subject of this report. Their value, however, extends far beyond analysis. They provide a framework for strategy design. What strategic elements do I need to research, think creatively around, make hard decisions about and eventually write down in my strategy document? In order to create a framework for strategy design, questions that would be asked by any designer in any field need to be answered. What is the purpose of the thing I am designing? And who am I designing for? The purpose of a strategy is, as discussed above, to bring about change. It therefore needs to be designed primarily for the change-makers. It needs to 'speak to' these individuals in words that will resonate for them. It needs to contain objectives they find meaningful and can take ownership of. Then the needs of the strategy's secondary audiences, the change-enablers (partner organisations, donors, funding bodies etc.) can be considered.

How Strategy Works

Finally, let's drill down into the practicalities of how a strategy affects change within an organisation. As we saw above, strategy is about choice. No organisation can do everything and certainly cannot do everything well. The difference between an organisation that has a strategy and one that doesn't is agreement about what is going to be done and what is not going to be done. For the choices made in a strategy to have an impact on the organisation, these choices need to be enacted, implemented or actioned in some way. University management has three main ways to ensure these choices make a difference:
1. Managing people: setting strategically-aligned performance criteria and reorganising teams, schools or faculties;
2. Setting policies, standards and methods of quality-control;
3. Preferential allocation of resources to support strategically chosen activities.

These do not need to be planned at an operational level of detail within university strategy but strategy needs to be sufficiently clear about the choices it makes to give clear, unambiguous guidance to operational planners. Any university strategy that fails to provide this clarity of guidance isn't fit for purpose.

2 UNIVERSITY STRATEGIES: OVERVIEW

The research for this report was conducted between December 2018 and February 2019, and involved an in-depth analysis of the published strategies of 52 UK universities and 28 one-to-one interviews with senior individuals with responsibility for, or influence over, university strategy.

All 52 universities studied had a public statement of some sort that could be seen as strategic. They varied from one university's 259-word statement on mission and values on a single web page to another university that had 34,600 words in 7 strategy documents over a total of 170 pages.

Figure 6 shows what the universities called their main strategy document.

Figure 6 Naming the strategy document

Of the seven strategies categorised above as 'Other", two were called [name of the university] + date (e.g. **Brunel** 2030), two were called [name of university] + vision + date (e.g. **Bath Spa University**'s Vision to 2020), one was called a 'Strategy Map', one was called 'Global Strategy' and one was called 'Mission and Core Values'.

One interesting question to arise from this analysis is whether there are any meaningful differences between documents labelled 'strategies' and documents labelled 'strategic plans'. One might imagine, for example, that a strategic plan might contain more planning information, such as KPIs and targets, than a strategy. The data, unfortunately, are inconclusive. 'Strategic Plans' contain KPIs more frequently: 59% of 'Strategic Plans' have KPIs compared to only 35% of 'Strategies' (a KPI is a dimension upon which success can be measured e.g. student satisfaction from the National Student Survey). 'Strategies' however, contain targets more frequently: 29% of 'Strategies' have targets compared to only 24% of 'Strategic Plans' (a target is a value used as a threshold to define success e.g. over 85% of students satisfied with the quality of their course in National Student Survey)

51 universities in our sample had a web page on their strategy, although this included the **University of Cambridge**'s page on its 'Mission and Core Values' (not strictly a strategy). Not all of these web pages were easy to find by search. For some universities, their functional or departmental strategies rank higher on Google than their institutional strategy. For other universities, a Google search still pointed to an old version of their strategy despite a new one having been published more than a month previously.

44 of our sample universities (85%) had a downloadable .pdf version of their strategy. Again these weren't always easy to find. One university had a link to their strategy pdf that required staff or student login to access it. There was however a publically available version on their website directly accessible from a Google search – it just wasn't linked from the strategy web page. 30 universities (58%) had at least an in-depth summary of their strategy, if not a full version of it, available as web content on one or more web pages on their website. This makes the content of strategy documents more readily accessible, and potentially more shareable, than having it only available in pdf format.

Four universities used an online brochure-viewer, such as Issuu[48] or Yudu[49] to view their strategy documents. For three of the four of these universities, this is simply an alternative way to view the strategy: they have .pdf and online versions. For one university, however, this is the only way to view the strategy, which is a significant limitation. It is, for example, almost impossible to read the whole strategy on a mobile phone. 10 universities (19%) provided an introductory video to their strategy.

Most university strategies covered a five-year time period (n=27); in the sample of 52 they ranged from three years to twenty years (Figure 7). Seven strategies did not specify the time period they covered.

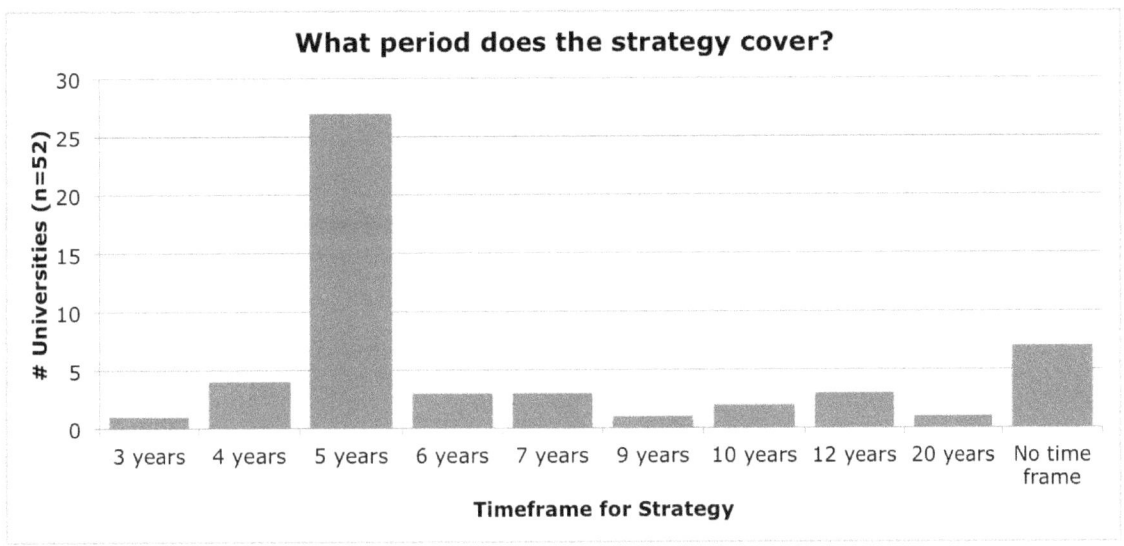

Figure 7 Timeframe for strategies

The length of university strategies varied considerably (Figure 8). The median word count was 3,267; the longest was 11,225.

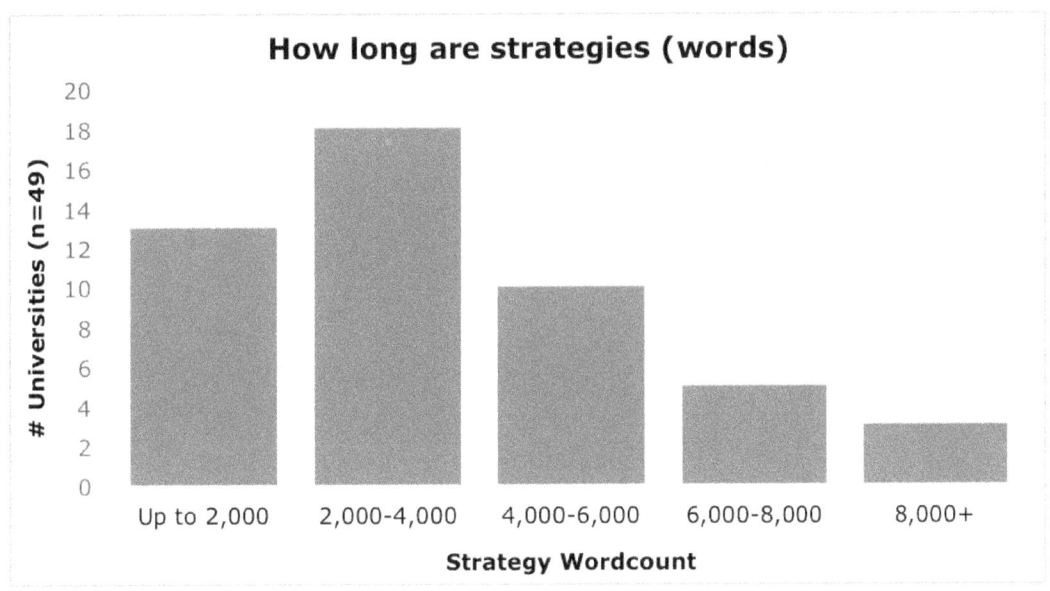

Figure 8 Strategy word counts

The median number of pages was 16 and the longest was 77 (Figure 9).

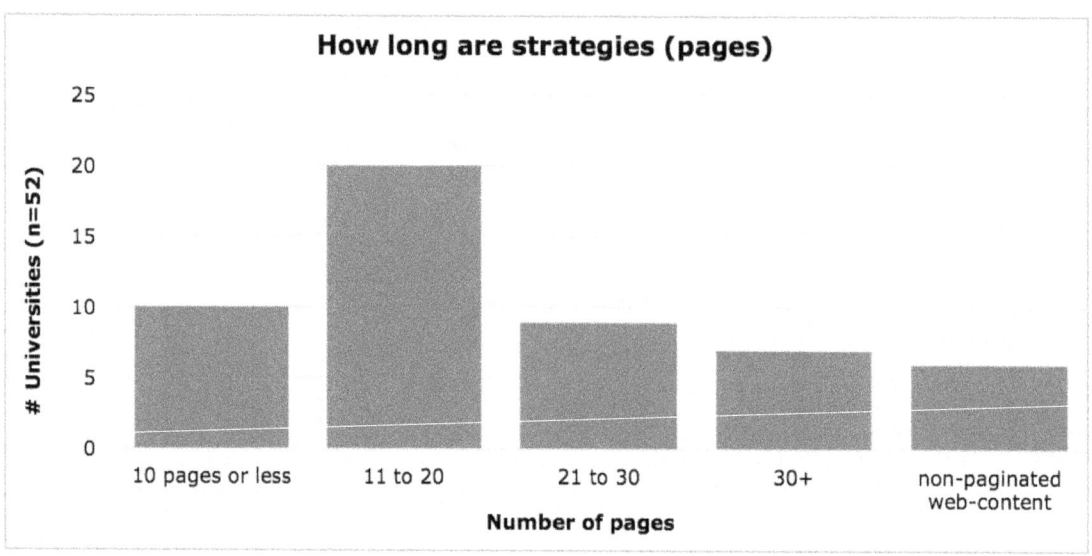

Figure 9 Strategy page numbers

Vision, Mission and Values

Most university strategies include* various combinations of vision, mission and values. 71% of our sample of university strategies included a vision statement, 62% included a mission statement and 65% included a statement of their values. 18 universities had all three and 4 didn't have vision, mission or values.

Table 1 'Vision', 'Mission' and 'Values'

	Vision	Mission	Values	Count	%
	✓	✓	✓	18	35%
	✓	✓	✗	8	15%
	✓	✗	✓	8	15%
	✗	✓	✓	3	6%
	✓	✗	✗	3	6%
	✗	✓	✗	3	6%
	✗	✗	✓	5	10%
	✗	✗	✗	4	8%
Totals	37	32	34	52	100%
%	71%	62%	65%		

* for this analysis we used the strict definition of 'inclusion' – the university themselves used the terms 'vision', 'mission' or 'values'

Let's explore these one at a time, starting with 'vision'.

Vision

As we saw in Chapter 1, vision is a picture of the organisation's potential;[50] it depicts what the organisation will look like in the future.[51] A good vision statement should be short, simple, specific to your business, leave nothing open to interpretation, and should have ambition.[52] It should be an audacious dream of a future reality based on the work you do.[53] It should inform, inspire and energise everyone in the organisation.[54] Of the 52 universities analysed for this report, 37 (71%) included a vision statement in their strategy. These vision statements refer to three distinct types of aspiration.

The first is about the university's status or reputation: they seek to be world-leading, world-class, a global leader, a leading university or the university of choice. Of these 37 visions, 27 (73%) of them had status- or reputation-based aspirations.

The second type of aspiration is social impact: they seek to transform the world, create better futures, make a difference to society or commit to the public good. A few were quite specific in this type of aspiration. **Aston University**, for example sought to equip "business and communities with the skills for future success". **Bangor University** sought to "ensure that our activities result in environmental benefit and social progress within a resilient economy". The **University of Nottingham** seeks to be "sustaining and improving the places and communities in which we are located [and] enhance industry, health and well-being, policy formation, culture and purposeful citizenship". Of the 37 visions, 19 of them (51%) had social-impact aspirations.

The third type of aspiration is student impact. A few vision statements sought to provide transformative education or sought to transform student outcomes. **Bath Spa University**'s vision, for example, says "Through inspirational teaching and research, we transform students' lives". A few talked about graduate outcomes, e.g. graduates of distinction or preparing graduates for their future. Others were specific in the student impact they sought. The **University of Bristol** sought to "nurture skilled, adaptable and resilient graduates". **Oxford Brookes University** sought to "educate confident citizens characterised by their generosity of spirit." **The University of Nottingham** sought to "develop skilled, reflective global citizens and leaders". Of the 37 visions, 18 of them (49%) had student-impact aspirations.

Table 2 shows how the universities combined these three different types of aspirations in their vision statements.

Table 2 Vision statements: types of aspiration

	University status / reputation	Social impact	Student impact	Count	%
	✓	✓	✓	5	14%
	✓	✓	✗	9	24%
	✓	✗	✓	7	19%
	✗	✓	✓	3	8%
	✓	✗	✗	5	14%
	✗	✓	✗	3	8%
	✗	✗	✓	3	8%
	✗	✗	✗	2	5%
Totals	27	19	18	37	100%
%	73%	51%	49%		

Mission

As we said in Chapter 1, mission is a statement of core purpose and focus that normally remains unchanged over time.[55] It answers the question, "Why does our business exist?"[56]. A mission statement communicates the organisation's purpose to its employees, customers, suppliers and other stakeholders and creates a sense of identity for its employees.[57]

Equating mission to purpose is handy because purpose can be defined simply as 'what you do that matters to others'. This pattern, 'what do you do?' and 'why does it matter to others?' can be seen repeatedly in the mission statements of the world's most distinctive brands[58]. **Google**'s mission is "To organize the world's information and make it universally accessible and useful.". What do they do? Organise the world's information. Why does it matter to others? It makes that information useful and accessible to everyone. **LinkedIn**'s mission is "To connect the world's professionals to make them more productive and successful." What do they do? Connect the world's professionals. Why does it matter to others? It makes those professionals more productive and successful. **Tripadvisor**'s mission is "To help people around the world plan and have the perfect trip." What do they do? Help people with travel planning. Why does it matter to others? So they can have the perfect trip. **Amazon**'s mission is "To be Earth's most customer-centric company, where customers can find and discover anything they might want to buy online, and endeavors to offer its customers the lowest possible prices." What do they do? Enable people to buy anything online. Why does it matter to others? Customers can find anything they want at the lowest possible prices. **Paypal**'s mission is "To build the Web's most convenient, secure, cost-effective payment solution." What do they do? Build online payment solutions. Why does it matter to others? It is convenient, secure and cost-effective. The **BBC**'s mission is "To enrich people's lives with programmes and services that inform, educate and entertain." What do they do? Make programmes and services. Why does it matter to others? It enriches viewers and listeners lives by informing, educating and entertaining them. **Medecins sans Frontieres**' mission is "To help people worldwide where the need is greatest, delivering emergency medical aid to people affected by conflict, epidemics, disasters or exclusion from health care." What do they do? Deliver emergency medical aid. Why does it matter to others? It helps people worldwide where need is greatest, due to conflict, epidemics, disasters or exclusion from health care. These are simple yet profound ways to capture the essence of an organisation.

Of the 32 universities that had a mission in their published strategies, 12 said that they mattered to others because they were going to 'benefit society', 'improve the world' or words to that effect. A few universities were more specific about why they mattered to others. The **University of Bath**'s mission sought to "educate students to become future leaders and innovators". **Kingston University**'s mission sought to "enhance students' life chances". **Solent University**'s mission sought to "promoting economic and social prosperity for the communities we serve" and **Swansea University** sought "to drive economic growth, foster prosperity, enrich the community and cultural life of Wales".

Values

As defined in Chapter 1, values are the ethical ideals of the organisation.[59] They are important and lasting beliefs or ideals shared by the members of a culture about what is good or bad and desirable or undesirable.[60]

Of the 52 universities analysed for this report, 34 strategies included statements of values. Of these 34, some universities adopted a narrative approach to defining their values. The **University of York**, for example, said "We apply the highest ethical standards to all our activities and want to make a positive contribution to the development of a fairer and sustainable world." 24 of the 34 universities with values in their strategy, by contrast, label their values with a single word (e.g. integrity) or a few words (e.g. academic freedom), making them easier to analyse. Within those 24 statements of values, a total of 58 different values were mentioned 145 times. The values mentioned 4 or more times in those 24 strategies are shown in Table 3.

Table 3 'Value' keywords

Value	Number of times mentioned in 24 university strategies
Inclusion	13
Excellence	12
Ambition	10
Integrity	7
Innovation	6
Professionalism	6
Respect	6
Collaboration	5
Community	4
Creativity	4
Diversity	4
Fairness	4
Sustainability	4

Content of Entire Strategy

In subsequent chapters we will explore how strategies are structured and what they contain in different parts of their structure. Before we leave this overview chapter, let's review the overall content of university strategies. To analyse this, each university strategy was, where possible, saved as a text-file (49 of 52 universities) and then all of the text files for these 49 strategies was combined into a single text file. This large file and the individual files for each university were then analysed using TagCrowd[61], an online word-cloud visualisation service. This displays the words in the submitted text file with font-size proportional to word frequency.

Figure 10 is a word-cloud of the words contained in all 49 strategies that were able to be text-mined for this report. Figures 11 to 13 show a sample of the word-clouds for individual universities, taking strategies from three universities.

academic achieve activities aim approach areas build business challenges change collaboration commitment **community** continue contribute create culture deliver **develop** diversity **education** effective employers enable encourage engagement enhance ensure enterprise environment **excellence experience** facilities future **global** graduates help higher **impact** improve including **increase** industry **innovation** institution **international** investment key **knowledge** leading **learning** level local national needs number offer **opportunities** partners **partnerships** people plan position priorities professional programmes provide public quality recognised region **research** resources school **services** skills social society **staff** strategic strategy **students** study success **support** sustainable teaching technology uk values vision **work** world years

Figure 10 Word-cloud from the combined text of 49 universities

achieve activities align **beneficiaries business** collaborative community continue **current** deliver development **education** engagement ensure **focus** future **graduate** group implementation increase international **key level local** outputs **offering** organisations **outcomes** partners partnerships performance professional **professions** quality **region research** resources sector skills **society staff** **strategy** strategies strong **students** success **support** teaching **values** work

Figure 11 Word-cloud from the text of the University of Aston strategy

Note the clear focus on beneficiaries in Figure 11, something the **University of Aston** mentions as being a distinctive feature of its strategy.

Figure 12 Word-cloud from the text of the De Montfort University strategy

Note the prominence of community in **De Montfort University**'s strategy (Figure 12).

Figure 13 Word-cloud from the text of the University of Oxford strategy

Clearly, research dominates all other words in the **University of Oxford**'s strategy (Figure 13).

We now return to the Strategy Design Framework (Figure 5) introduced in Chapter 1. The eight elements of the Strategy Design Framework (Destination, Methods, Alignment, Innovation, Priority, Performance, Agility and Adoption) that every good strategy should contain will now be explored in turn in the chapters that follow.

3 STRATEGY ELEMENT: DESTINATION

Where are we striving to get to?

According to Roger Martin "Strategy is ... one integrated set of choices: what is our winning aspiration?"[62] Richard Rumelt says "A good strategy [sets out] to accomplish an important end ... instead [of having] multiple goals and initiatives that symbolize progress, but no coherent approach to accomplishing that progress."[63]

Many universities appear to agree, to the extent that they emphasise the importance of being distinctive as part of their strategies.

- The **University of York** says simply "we aim to build a University that distinguishes itself."
- The **University of Bath** seeks to "enhance the distinctive characteristics of our research and teaching excellence."
- The **University of Chester** says "for us to continue to be a successful university we recognise that we have to offer innovative and exciting programmes of study within a distinctive learning environment."
- The **University of Lincoln** aims to have "a distinctive reputation for its research which we can now develop and build further ... [and] a distinctive approach to education through partnership and engagement with our students and our external partners.
- **University College London's** vision is: "Our distinctive approach to research, education and innovation will further inspire our community of staff, students and partners to transform how the world is understood, how knowledge is created and shared and the way that global problems are solved."
- "**Aston University**'s strategy gives us the opportunity to identify our points of distinction," according to the Vice Chancellor in his introduction to the strategy. Aston's strategy goes on to expand "to be a successful university in the future, we

will need to be more distinctive" and "We have the opportunity to reinforce and build on these existing strengths and differentiate ourselves from our competitors."
- **Brighton University** talks about "what makes us different", whilst its near neighbour, the **University of Sussex** proclaims it will "Dare to be Different"
- **University of Northampton** says in its strategy that "UK higher education has become a crowded 'Red Ocean', increasingly competitive and for some, resource restricted. In order to thrive we must keep on seeking opportunities in uncontested (Blue Ocean) space."

Many university strategies fall into the multiple-goals-and-initiatives trap that Rumelt urges us to avoid. One university, for example, has a section in its strategy all about its distinction. It contains 4 goals with 17 initiatives to achieve them. There is no mention of the 'winning aspiration' or the 'important end' that all this effort is directed towards. There is nothing to suggest that a particular synergy is expected to emerge from the combination of these specific activities. There is nothing to enable them to all pull together and nothing to stop them all pulling in opposite directions. It hardly amounts to a single, coherent and memorable destination!

Of the few universities that did clarify their strategic destination, they adopted quite different approaches to doing so. The **University of Sussex**, for example, simply declares its aspiration to be "disruptive by design" and explains that the University was originally "designed to be different [and] has a distinguished tradition of disruptive and experimental interventions." Sussex then drills down into what this means for education: "Sussex students will develop the knowledge and skills to be critical thinkers, entrepreneurs, commentators, citizens and activists" and research: "We will challenge conventional thinking and discourses, offering inspiring and creative ways to understand and solve global issues."

For **De Montfort University** the 'destination' for its strategy and its vision are the same thing. Under the heading 'Vision' they say "By 2023, our unsurpassed commitment to the public good and transformational scholarship will position us as the definition of a 21st century global university." Since their strategy runs to 2023, this means they plan to achieve their vision by means of this strategy. This raises an interesting philosophical question; isn't vision something more enduring than the period covered by a single strategy? It also raises the very practical issue that success in the current strategy would commit the author of the next strategy to invent a whole new vision for the organisation.

The **University of Northampton** comments specifically about the relationship between its previous strategy (2010-2015) and current strategy (2015-2020). "In Raising the Bar we set out to become the number one university in the UK for Social Enterprise by 2015. We achieved this ambition. For 2015 – 2020 Social Impact (social value creation) provides an expanded narrative and logical progression that transcends our previous goal." Social impact is defined as "the cumulative positive effects of the University on the social and economic fabric, health and wellbeing of communities we serve." So, they have moved from a strategy 'destination' that previously was simple, clear, precise and highly differentiating to one that is, in their words, 'expanded'. And perhaps they felt they had to do so because becoming "the number one university in the UK for Social Enterprise" was made the 'destination' for a specific strategy rather than being a longer-term, over-arching 'vision'.

The **University of Salford** is clear that it aims to avoid such issues. They have a vision: "By pioneering exceptional industry partnerships we will lead the way in real world experiences preparing students for life." This vision, they claim, "will bring enormous benefits to students, staff and industry partners. To deliver these benefits we are engaged in developing Industry Collaboration Zones as our single institution-wide Strategic Priority over the five years of this strategy."

It is clear, both from our analysis of published strategies and our interviews with university leaders that this is an issue they struggle with. There are inevitable difficulties in finding a strategic destination that will equally inspire a teacher, a researcher, a student and a member of professional support staff; that will resonate equally for a physicist, a historian and a sociologist.

This is less of a challenge the more specialist your university is. The **University of the Arts London** and the **Royal Academy of Music** were included in our sample of universities to explore issues such as this. Interestingly, however, neither depended solely on their specialism to define their strategic destination.

The **University of the Arts London** seeks to provide "transformational education for the creative world" with the addition that they value "traditional tools and workshops as much as emerging technology."

The **Royal Academy of Music** aims to provide "musical training at the highest international, professional standards" and also seeks to be "conservatoire of choice for top global talent aspiring to a successful, creative, professional career."

For all universities, the issue of strategic destination also plays squarely into the 'competition versus collaboration' debate. Should my strategy be founded upon working with other universities for the common good or defeating them in a competitive marketplace? The answer, as is hopefully clear from the strategy excerpts above, is that strategy destination is about a lot more than competitive advantage.

Key recommendations for 'destination' within university strategies:

1. Strategies with a single, simple, clear 'destination' will be a lot more memorable than those with multiple complex goals.
2. Strategies with a single, tangible, specific 'destination' will be intrinsically more focused and will also enable more focused strategic decision-making. 'Which of these plausible alternatives will be more effective in getting us closer to our strategic destination?'
3. "Start with people!" This is Roger Martin and AG Lafley's advice for finding the high-order aspiration for an organisation.[64] What matters to our customers? What engages and motivates our staff (see 4 below)?

4. Good strategies give staff a coherent sense of purpose that engages and motivates them. Teresa Amabile's research[65] shows that a sense of tangible progress towards a meaningful purpose makes employees motivated and engaged at work more than pay, more than a good working relationship with their boss, more than praise and recognition.
5. Try to separate the destination of any particular strategy from the longer-term vision for the organisation. Vision and values are what should provide stability and continuity across strategies.
6. Remember that strategy destination is one part of the eight-piece jigsaw that makes up the Strategy Design Framework. A good destination is, therefore, one that will be reached by a small number of core methods working in concert. A good destination is one that aligns well with the obstacles and opportunities presented by the university's operating environment AND aligns well with the evolving needs of university customers AND aligns well with the university's potential to transform. A good destination is one that supports innovation and forms part of a strategy that can be readily adopted by stakeholders.

4 STRATEGY ELEMENT: METHODS

Core activities to reach our destination

A core principle at the heart of several contemporary theories of strategy is that strategic focus needs to be tightly integrated with enabling actions.

Sull et al suggest "Strategic priorities should be forward-looking and action-oriented and should focus attention on the handful of choices that matter most to the organization's success over the next few years."[66] Figure 14 shows their analysis of the variety of terms used by S&P 500 companies to describe the handful of key actions designed to implement their strategy.

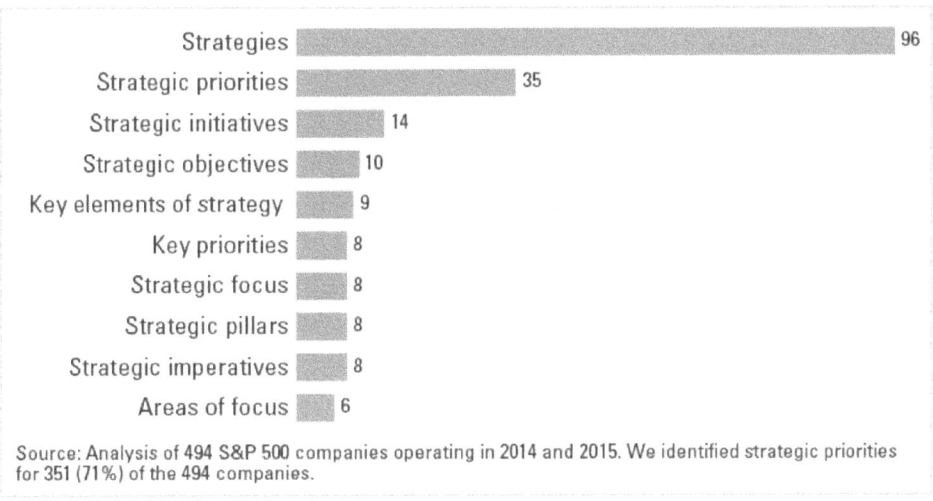

Figure 14 Key actions to implement strategy (Sull et al, 2018)

Richard Rumelt argues that "A good strategy includes a set of coherent actions. They are not "implementation" details; they are the punch in the strategy."[67] He goes on: "Good strategy is coherent action backed up by an argument, an effective mixture of thought and action [containing] a set of coherent actions ... coordinated with one another to work together."[68]

Donald Sull and Kathleen Eisenhartd use the term 'simple rules' to describe "a powerful weapon against the complexity that threatens to overwhelm individuals [and] organisations. [Simple rules] ... are limited to a few ... are tailored to the organization using them ... apply to a well-defined activity or decision ... provide clear guidance while conferring the latitude to exercise discretion."[69]

So we start, as described in Chapter 3, with the strategy 'Destination'. It is the winning aspiration, the important end or the coherent account of where we are striving to get to. Then we move on to how are we going to get there. What are the handful of choices, the set of coherent actions, the few simple rules that together are pivotal to bringing about strategic success? We call them the strategy's 'Methods', i.e. the core activities needed to reach our destination.

The 52 university strategies analysed for this report use a myriad of different labels for these Methods. The **University of Bristol** has eight "Cornerstones of our Strategy". The **University of Liverpool** has four "Goals". The **University of Northampton** has four "Critical Success Factors". The **University of Leicester** has four "Key Pillars of Activity", whilst the **University of Derby** has merely "Pillars". The **University of the Arts London** has "Strategic Areas", whilst the **University of Sussex** merely has "Areas".

A total of 41 university strategies were found to have content that could be text-mined and that had Methods with identifiable labels. Analysing these (Figure 15), we found that the most common adjective used was strategic (in 14 strategies) and the most common noun was priority (in 8 strategies).

Figure 15 Adjectives / nouns describing 'Methods'

The number of Methods they had in their strategy varied from three to eight (Figure 16).

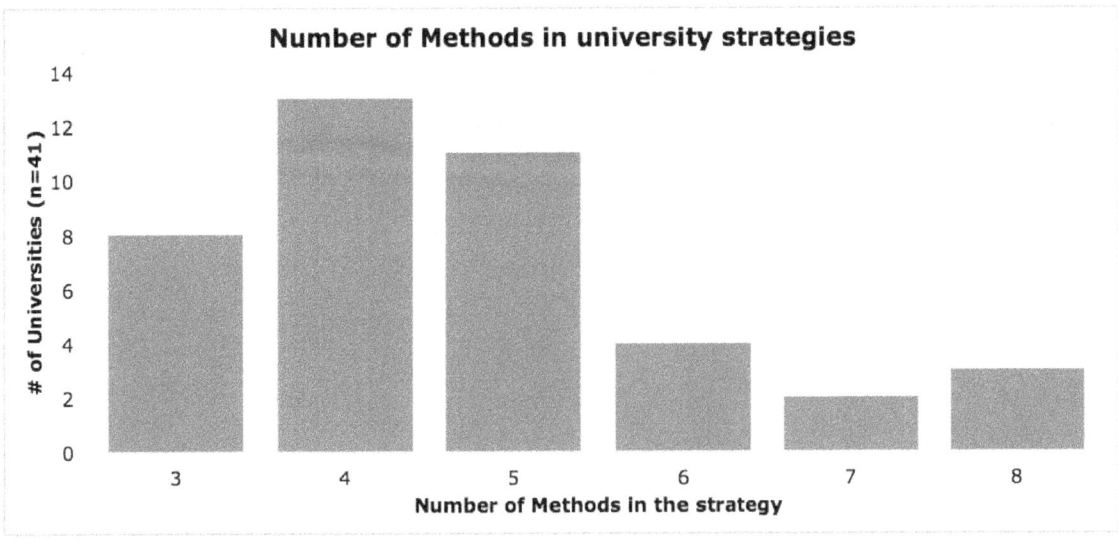

Figure 16 Number of Methods in university strategies

This analysis does not include seven universities who presented their methods in two clusters. The **University of Bangor**, for example have four "Strategic Priorities" and five "Strategic Enablers". **Robert Gordon University** has four "Aims" and four "Enablers". The **University of Nottingham** has two "Core Strategies" and two "Enabling Strategies".

Key recommendations for 'methods' within university strategies:

1. University strategies need to identify a handful of methods that, together, will be pivotal to achieving strategic success (to get to the strategy destination).
2. Methods need to be both sufficient and necessary to achieve the strategy destination.

5 STRATEGY ELEMENT: ALIGNMENT

The logic connecting actions to outcomes

Richard Rumelt argues that "A good strategy honestly acknowledges the challenges being faced and provides an approach to overcoming them."[70] In other words, strategy aligns internal response to external challenges. Specifically, strategy needs to ensure employees are proficient at the internal processes needed to provide services to customers in ways that are distinctive from competitors (Figure 17).

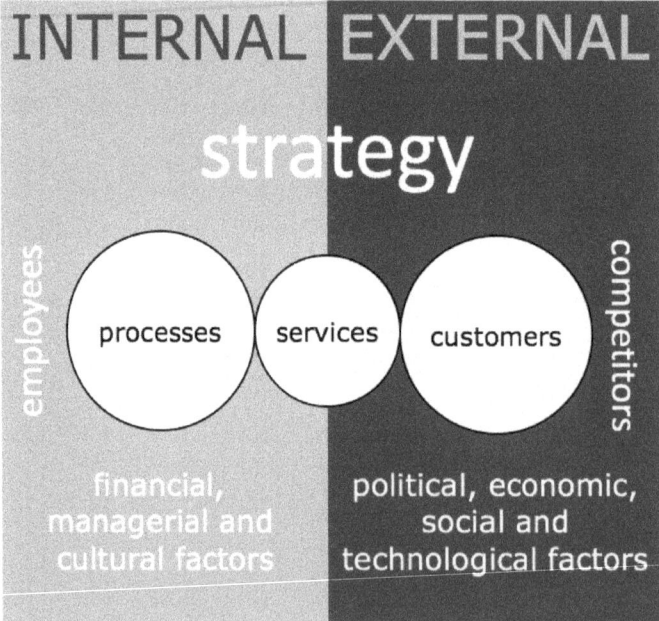

Figure 17 Strategy needs to ensure that employees are proficient at the internal processes needed to provide services to customers in ways that are distinctive to competitors

Figure 18 shows a framework for strategy alignment.

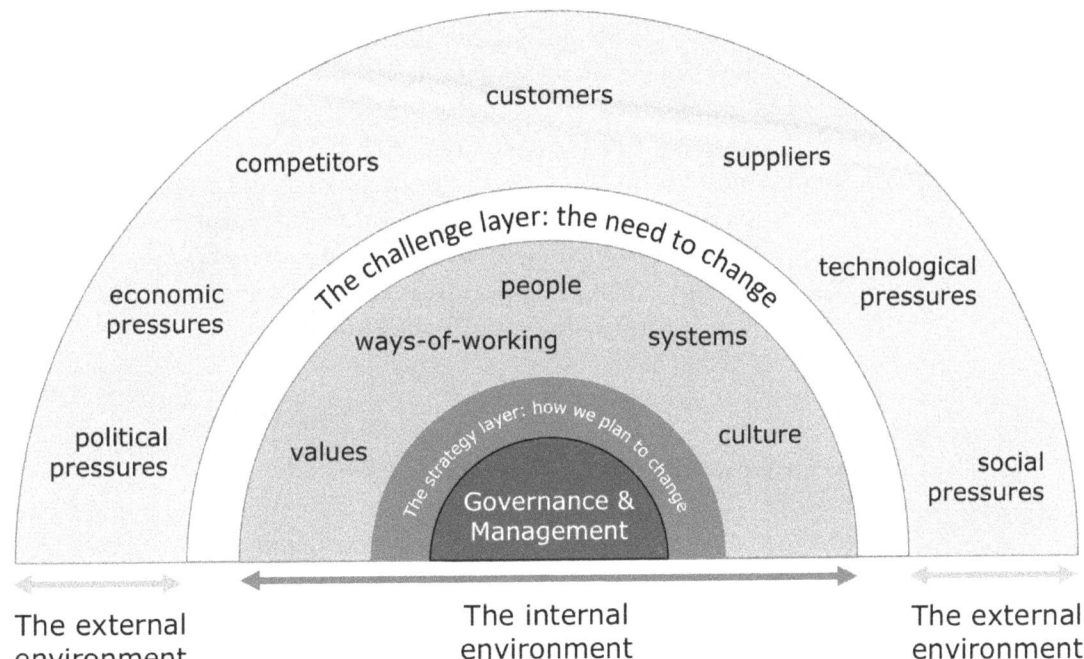

Figure 18 Goal Atlas's framework for strategy alignment

To be effective, a strategy needs to be aligned with:
1. **The organisation's external operating environment.**
    a. Customers – the most obvious customers for universities are its students but other people and organisations that pay money to universities also need to be included. Mostly these will include Government funding bodies but may also include private organisations buying services (e.g. research) and individual benefactors. The importance of aligning strategy with the interests of benefactors was made vividly clear to the **University of St Andrews** when the parents of a former student pledged £10M on the condition that the money was used purely to carry out the vision laid out in the University's newly published strategy.[71]
    b. Competitors – clearly, other universities are competitors but they are not the only ones. For example, commercial organisations, especially start-ups, are encroaching on the traditional university marketplace (e.g. online learning from companies such as Udemy, Coursera, FutureLearn).
    c. Suppliers – the more universities outsource their operations to external suppliers, the more they will depend on those suppliers to deliver elements of their strategy. The bigger commercial suppliers of university services take

their clients' strategies seriously. As part of this research we analysed the full range of strategy documents published by a few universities. One of these universities had a main institutional strategy and six sub-strategies. Of those six sub-strategies only one referred to the main strategy and made the effort to align tightly with that main strategy: it was the one strategy written by a commercial supplier of services to the university.

d. Political, economic, social and technological (PEST) pressures – several of the interviewees for this report said that identifying and working out how to respond to these pressures was the hardest part of strategy management. The Augar review[72] of 2018, demographic change (e.g. the recent dip in numbers of 18 year olds) and changes to performance assessment (e.g. Teaching Excellence and Student Outcomes Framework, Research Excellence Framework, Knowledge Exchange Framework) all herald potential changes in university funding that will require strategic response.

2. **The internal environment within the organisation.**
    a. Operations: people, process, technology and data. Strategy should recognise and honour current ways of working and then identify and justify the changes needed to respond to external pressures. A great approach to engaging and aligning operational teams with strategy, across the strategy lifecycle, is provided by the VW strategy alignment framework[73] (Figure 19).

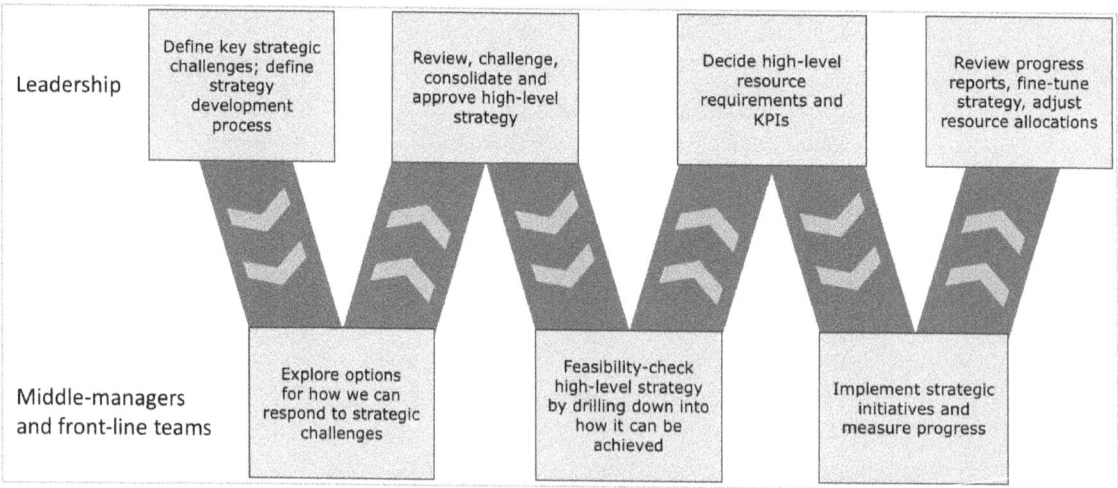

Figure 19 The VW framework shows the steps in a combined top-down and bottom-up approach to the alignment of strategy and operations

b. The need to change and potential for change. As mentioned in Chapter 1, change is disruptive, expensive, hard work and often stressful to those

making it happen. It should be sought sparingly and only ever for good reasons. A well-designed strategy will align what needs to change with why it needs to change and also how it is proposed to change.
   c. Culture and values. Some universities attach great importance to their heritage. The **University of Liverpool**, for example, has had the same mission since 1881: "the advancement of learning and the ennoblement of life". The **University of Sussex** celebrates a different heritage – "a distinguished tradition of disruptive and experimental interventions" and aligns its entire strategy around "dare to be different" and "disruptive by design".

3. **Governance and management.**
   a. Audit and oversight. Many university strategies are explicit about how they will be governed. The **University of Dundee**, for example says "Progress is regularly reviewed by University Executive Group and Court." In such a turbulent period for universities, there is likely to be a trend towards closer and more strict oversight of strategies, in which case a formal strategy audit[74] might be considered. This is an independent, evidence-based review of the process by which the strategy was developed, a review of the output from that process (usually one or more strategy documents) and a review of the processes for implementing, supporting and measuring the strategy. However audit and oversight are achieved, strategy must be aligned with the means of governing it. There is no point in having weekly progress updates in a strategic initiative that will take 5 years to complete. Nor is there any point in having annual reports on an initiative due to be completed in 9 months. Equally, if a strategic initiative is known to involve significant risk, the oversight of that initiative needs to be risk-aware.
   b. Strategy implementation. A strategy is an action-plan. A strategy is, therefore, only fit-for-purpose if it is actionable. Aligning the need for strategic change with the need for feasible strategy implementation is a delicate task. Most proposals for change receive pushback from someone claiming it is too difficult. This is where a model such as the VW framework (Figure 19) can be so powerful in aligning the change-leaders with the change-makers.
   c. Strategy resourcing. Bringing about change is expensive. It requires people with dedicated time to invent and refine new ways of working. Those new ways of working may require new technology or new data in order to work effectively. Once devised, these new ways of working will need to be embedded and integrated into adjacent ways of working and the organisation's systems and processes. All this will require coordination and facilitation for which dedicated management time will be needed. So for

change to happen, resources need to be found. Strategy therefore needs to be aligned with the means of delivering success.

    d. Performance management and control. In the interviews we conducted for this report, we heard from many people that financial planning had matured significantly in the university sector over the past 5 years. The planning cycle was better established, planning horizons were no longer limited to the following year and forecasting was becoming more evidence-based. This lays the groundwork for both the development of more evidence-based strategies and the more meaningful measurement of strategic progress. This, perhaps, makes it even more important that strategies are aligned with the means and metrics of their measurement.

4. **Strategy's alignment with … strategy**
    a. Strategy's internal consistency. Internal inconsistencies are what we have come to call the hidden trap of strategy. A strategy can read well, can look like it all hangs together yet still fall apart when examined in more detail. One university strategy, for example, says that it "expects excellence" from its staff. It then explains how it will value, build, recognise and reward excellence. It says nothing, however, about what they will do if, despite all their valuing, building, recognising and rewarding, some staff fail to achieve excellence. Is excellence expected or merely encouraged? To say it is expected, yet only explain how it is going to be encouraged, is a strategic misalignment.
    b. The nested strategy cascade. Many universities have multiple strategies. The **University of Dundee** has its main University Strategy[75], supported by an Estates Strategy[76] and a Retention and Progression Strategy[77]. The **University of York** has its main University Strategy[78], supported by a Teaching and Learning Strategy, a Research Strategy, an International Strategy, a Student Mental Health and Well-Being Strategy, a Student and Academic Services Strategy, a Sustainability Strategy and an Equality, Diversity and Inclusion Strategy. A total of six supporting strategies.[79] This clearly could be a source of considerable strategic mis-alignment. Recognising this issue, Lafley and Martin say in larger organisations there are "multiple levels of choices and interconnected [strategies] … The result is a set of nested cascades that cover the full organisation."[80] The concept of cascade is critical. The top-most strategy, in our case the strategy for the entire university, defines the external challenges, the high-level actions to be taken in response and then reconcile how to make this strategy fit-for-implementation. This sets the focus and boundaries that need to apply to every sub-strategy. The choices made in the top strategy need to cascade down into every subordinate strategy. Likewise the choices made in every

one of these second-tier strategies need to cascade down to any third-tier strategy. So, for example a University Strategy sets the focus and boundaries for a Teaching and Learning Strategy. A Teaching and Learning Strategy sets the focus and boundaries for an Assessment Strategy.

How to align: an introduction to Goal Mapping

Having discussed what needs to be aligned in a well-designed strategy, let us now turn our attention to how we align. Richard Rumelt hinted at the solution when he said "Good strategy is not just "what" you are trying to do. It is also "why" and "how" you are doing it."[81] Finding a systematic way to join up the hows and whys of strategy will provide us with our alignment methodology.

Fortunately just such a methodology has been around for a very long time. It was invented in 1947 by Larry Miles[82] of the General Electric Company. Miles was an engineer in a purchasing department of General Electric at a time when industry was booming but growth was constrained by post-war shortages of materials. There was a general need to do more with less. This prompted Miles to start asking purchasing questions in a different way from usual. Rather than asking his suppliers to price things, he asked them to price functions, the purpose the things were intended to serve. So rather than pricing nuts and bolts he asked them to price a way of fixing two items together. This became known as value analysis or value engineering[83] and Larry Miles, to this day, is recognised as its founder[84]. Soon the growth of value analysis generated demand for standardised ways of analysing the functions that products or components served: and so functional analysis was born.[85]

Function analysis is a way of mapping how the different functions served by a product or service interconnect. The result is a logic diagram arranged so that higher order functions are at the top of the diagram and cascade down to progressively lower order functions. Figure 20[86] shows a simple analysis of the functions of a corkscrew.

If, instead of product functions we think more generally of goals, we have a tool for strategy alignment.

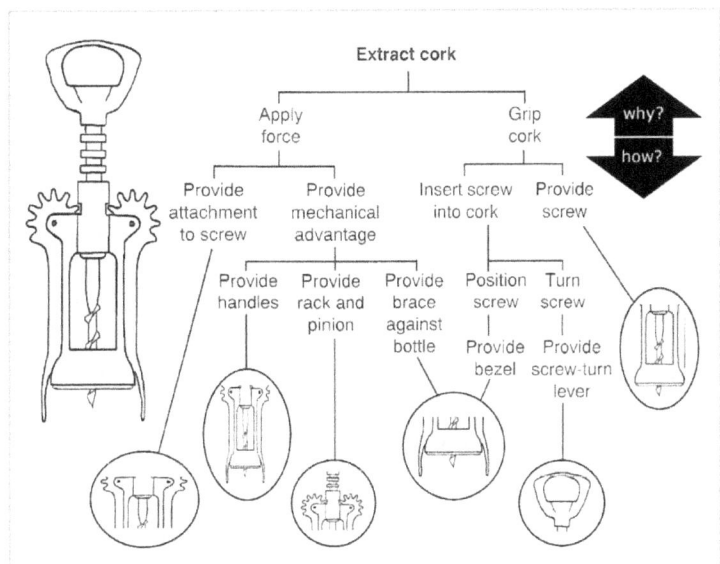

Figure 20 Function analysis of a corkscrew

Let's explore this by goal-mapping the **University of Glasgow** strategy (Figure 21).

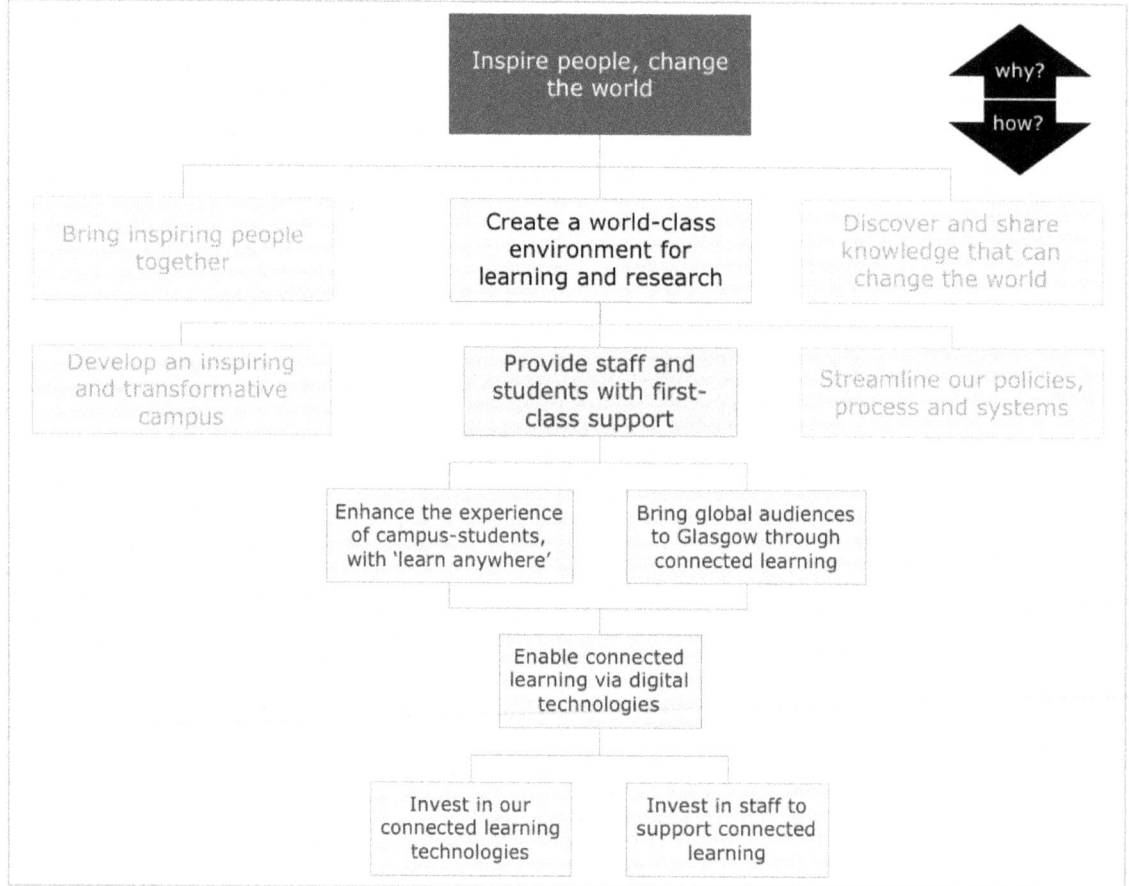

Figure 21 A goal map of part of the University of Glasgow strategy

As we move from top to bottom of the goal map we repeatedly answer the question 'how?' How are we going to inspire people and change the world? By creating a world-class environment for learning and research. How are we going to create that world-class environment? By providing staff and students with first-class support. How do we provide that first-class support? By enhancing the experience of campus-students with learn-anywhere. How do we support learn anywhere? By enabling connected learning via digital technologies. How do we enable connected learning? By investing in both technology and staff support.

We can also move up through the goal map with the question 'why?'. Why are we investing in connected learning technologies? In order to enable connected learning. Why do we want connected learning? In order to enhance the experience of campus students. Why do we want to enhance student experience? In order to inspire people and change the world. What this goal mapping reveals is that the **University of Glasgow** strategy has a strong core method (create a world class environment for learning and research) that drills down logically to investments in technology and people. It also highlights potential gaps in the strategy. Connected technologies alone will not bring global audiences to Glasgow.

Key recommendations for 'alignment' within university strategies:

1. Alignment is vital in strategy. It is what makes everyone pull in the same direction instead of pulling in different directions and making no impact.
2. There is a lot to align in a well-designed strategy: customers, competitors, suppliers as well as political and economic disruptors in the external operating environment; people, systems, ways-of-working, culture, values, governance and management in the internal environment.
3. Strategy also needs internal consistency and, where appropriate, consistency between any sub-strategies.
4. Goal mapping provides a rigorous, logical way to explore and validate the alignment of component parts of a strategy.

6 STRATEGY ELEMENT: INNOVATION

The cultivation of new ways of thinking and working

Since strategy is about change and change is usually driven by innovation, it is not surprising that most universities refer to innovation extensively in their strategies.

How many times does innovation* (Figure 22: *and related words with the same word stem, such as innovations, innovative, innovator) appear in the 52 university strategies analysed?

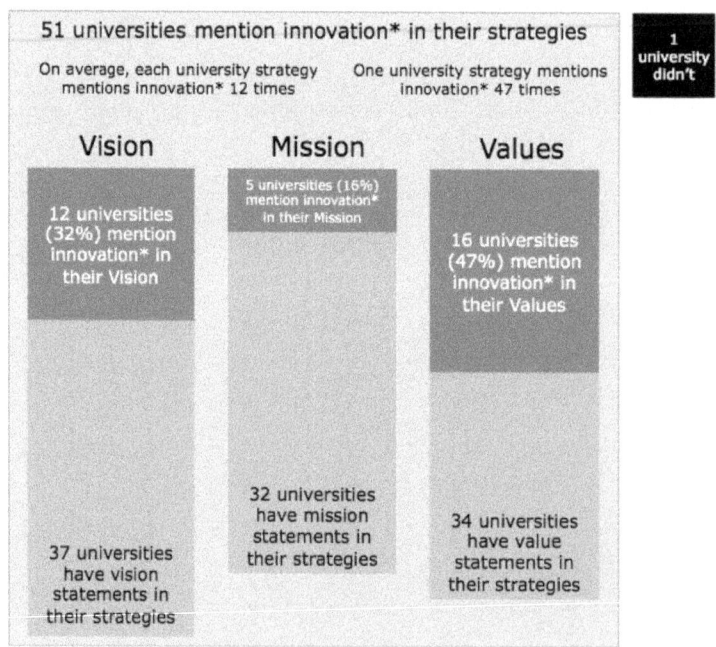

Figure 22 Prevalence of 'innovation' keywords in university strategies

A key indicator of bad strategy, according to Richard Rumelt, is 'fluff'. "Fluff is a superficial restatement of the obvious combined with a generous sprinkling of buzzwords. Fluff masquerades as expertise, thought, and analysis. As a simple example of fluff in strategy work, here is a quote from a major retail bank's internal strategy memoranda: "Our fundamental strategy is one of customer-centric intermediation." The Sunday word (a word that is inflated and unnecessarily abstruse) "intermediation" means that the company accepts deposits and then lends them to others. In other words, it is a bank."[87]

When it comes to innovation, university strategies contain a lot of fluff. Here are a few examples from seven different university strategies:

- "We will find innovative solutions to the challenges faced by humankind"
- "Our discoveries and innovations will shape business and enterprise for the 21st century"
- "Our outstanding research feeds our burgeoning reputation for innovation, creativity and impact"
- "Our innovation enables us to accelerate economic growth and social advances"
- "Our research deliverables will lead to innovation in industry and public policy"
- "Our innovation is focused on making a practical, positive difference to people's lives"
- "We are committed to developing staff and students to their full potential to produce a vibrant and innovative community"
- "We are innovative and creative; continually evolving, never standing still"
- "Research and innovation will become central to all our activities"
- "Innovative curriculum design will maintain the recognised quality of our delivery"
- "Our learning and teaching will deliver innovative approaches which meet the needs of our students"
- "We will be innovative in our use of technology to support the operation of efficient and effective systems"

Whilst these range from grandiose to practical, they all sound impressive but say little. They fail to define the nature of the innovation and don't explain how the innovation will be pursued.

In a well-designed strategy innovation should be defined by answering these four questions:

1. **Why do we need to innovate?** Innovation is notoriously expensive and risky[88] and hence needs to be robustly justified within a strategy.
2. **What are we intending to change?** Often this will be a change in our processes or ways of working (e.g. partner with regional enterprises to make our research more industry-relevant). It may however refer to the inputs into those ways of working (e.g. the adoption of digital technologies for teaching and learning), or

the outputs from those ways of working (e.g. make our graduates more employable).

3. **How will we innovate? / who will innovate?** This is the strategic part of innovation – how are we going to make it happen? Typically, this will be about people, process or resources.
4. **How will we know if the innovation has been successful?** Ideally this should be defined strategically (to what extent will we be better prepared to overcome the challenges we face?) and analytically (which KPIs will be taken to indicate innovation success?).

Here are three good examples from university strategies:

1. Despite the fact that its core teaching methods (the tutorial method of teaching) have existed at the university since the 11th century,[89] the **University of Oxford** has found a nice balance between tradition/heritage and strategic innovation. Oxford's vision is to "build on the University's long-standing traditions of independent scholarship and academic freedom while fostering a culture in which innovation and collaboration play an important role." They describe their approach to teaching and learning as follows: "Through a commitment to the personal education of each student, we will provide a quality of education and experience which equips students with the values, skills and intellectual discipline that will enable them to make a positive contribution to society."
    - **Why do they need to innovate?** "To …refresh the University's rich academic environment" and "We are committed to innovation and excellence in teaching."
    - **What are they intending to change?** "…ensure that teaching is informed by best practice …[develop] an inclusive approach to learning … [and exploit] opportunities for innovation offered by digital technology."
    - **How will they innovate?** "[improve] our academic staff recognition and reward processes … encourage the development of new and innovative courses and fields of study"
    - **How will they know if the innovation has been successful?** Their "portfolio reflects advances in knowledge and meets the needs of today's students".

2. **Imperial College London's** mission is "to achieve enduring excellence in research and education in science, engineering, medicine and business for the benefit of society."
    - **Why do they need to innovate?** "We will act courageously and innovatively when pursuing new opportunities … we need to take academic and financial

risks to sustain excellence in research and education ... as the frontiers of knowledge cannot be predicted, agility and flexibility are integral attributes for success."

- **What are they intending to change?** "... starting new areas of research, before we know whether funding or acclaim will follow."
- **How will they innovate?** "We will adjust our processes so that we can make swift, informed decisions to seize opportunities and both start and stop new initiatives. We will invest funds to pursue the new and risky. We will support ideas which are potential breakthrough programmes that put us in a leadership position, even if these ideas have not yet received outside funding."
- **How will they know if the innovation has been successful?** "We have launched initiatives which have subsequently led to outside support."

3. **Solent University** offers "practical and professional education; our distinctive courses are uniquely tailored to industry needs".
   - **Why do they need to innovate?** Solent's vision is to become "the 'applied' university for the ... region ... [with] sector-leading integration of theory and practice ... in support of 'real world' learning."
   - **What are they intending to change?** "we intend to make a step-change in our commitment to research and innovation with the expectation that all of our academic staff will be involved in applied research or knowledge transfer by 2020."
   - **How will they innovate?** "We will strengthen our research infrastructure in order to support our academic staff, establishing a new Research and Innovation Office ... [expand] our programme of training for research supervisors, co-ordinate our support for external research funding bids, improve our arrangements for commercialising intellectual property and promote further knowledge transfer projects and contract research. Our staff commitment to research and innovation will be facilitated by enabling policies, processes and working practices. Similarly, we will ensure that students are exposed to research throughout their time at the University and that they have opportunities to be involved or engaged in research on a regular basis. Research informed activity will be a characteristic from induction to graduation."
   - **How will they know if the innovation has been successful?** "Annual increase in the proportion of academic staff with high quality research outputs or knowledge transfer partnerships; annual increase of external research income; annual increase of income from contract research, consultancy and services to business and the community."

All three of these examples bring innovation to life in a meaningful, coherent and practical way. These strategies immediately tell their reader what needs to change, why it needs to change and what is planned (and approved!) for the change to be brought about.

Key recommendations for 'innovation' within university strategies:

1. Make sure innovation is included – how will strategy drive change without it?
2. Think carefully about how much innovation your strategy requires. The bolder and more radical the strategy, the more innovation will be needed. The more innovation that is needed:
    a. the more resources will be needed to support it;
    b. the more disruptive it will be to the university's standard ways of working;
    c. the more risk there will be of innovation-failure, and possibly, as a result, of failure to meet strategic objectives.
3. Make sure innovation is defined in terms of:
    a. Why is innovation needed? How does it align with the rest of the strategy?
    b. What innovation is needed? Which aspect of the university needs to change and in what ways?
    c. How will the innovation be pursued? What initiatives or resources will support the innovation? How will we work differently to be innovative? Who is charged with leading the innovation?
    d. How will we know if the innovation has been successful? What success criteria or success metrics will be used to define success?
4. Make sure your strategy development process has a rigorous 'fluff-filter' around innovation.

7 STRATEGY ELEMENT: PRIORITY

The identification of what really matters

Strategy is all about choosing what to do in preference to the things you have chosen not to do. As a consequence, it is not surprising that the issue of priorities features prominently in university strategies. The 46 university strategies that we could do text analysis on mentioned priority (and other words with the word-stem 'priori') 226 times: an average of just under 5 mentions of priority per strategy. Priorities are referred to in four different ways.

Firstly they are referred to in a conversational way. The Vice Chancellor of **Anglia Ruskin University**, for example, says "If we are to succeed in delivering on our plans, we must prioritise." The **University of Sussex** strategy says "By working towards a shared vision, and having an understanding of our common goals, we will prioritise our efforts." The **University of Sheffield** strategy quotes an attendee at a science festival: "I thought it was absolutely fantastic that the University had decided to consult with the community about their priorities for research."

Secondly, 'priorities' refer to external strategies that inform or shape the university strategy. The **University of Surrey** identifies a future challenge to be "funding [being] increasingly targeted towards government priorities, for example those described in the Government's industrial strategy". **Queens University Belfast** notes that "Developing a prosperous, strong, and competitive regional economy is a key priority in the Northern Ireland Executive's Programme for Government". **Bangor University** strategy says "We will include a strong emphasis on research which has commercial and applied potential to support regional economic and policy priorities".

Thirdly, 'priorities' are used in the titles of elements of strategy documents. As we saw in Chapter 4 (Figure 15), eight universities label the core methods of their strategy as 'priorities'. **King's College London** has "Five Priorities to Deliver our Strategic Vision". The **University of Warwick** has two core purposes of Research and Education, which, its strategy says, "will be underpinned by four strategic priorities: Innovation, Inclusion, Regional Leadership and Internationalisation". The **University of Liverpool** strategy, for example, has five main sections, in each of which is a sub-section titled "Goals: What are Our Core Priorities and Objectives".

Finally and most importantly, university strategies 'set' priorities. In order to set a priority three questions must be answered:

1. What, exactly, is the priority being set? If, for example a strategy seeks to prioritise research, is it all research, research in specific disciplines, research directed towards particular types of impact or research by younger academics? Also, what priority is being given? Is it top priority in the entire strategic plan or third priority or tenth priority? If there are five strategic priorities with no differentiation in their ranking how are decisions to be made about which wins or loses in competition for scarce resources?
2. Why is this priority being set? This is largely a question of alignment. How will this priority contribute to overall strategic success? Is this priority expected to work in synergy with, or in support of, another priority? What was it about this priority that made it more important than the other alternatives that failed to be prioritised?
3. How is this priority being prioritised? Is it going to have the most resources invested in it? Will it take longest to make an impact and hence needs to be started first? Or is it expected to deliver the biggest benefit and hence needs to be managed most carefully?

How well do university strategies manage priorities? The **University of Warwick** strategy talks a lot about priorities. As mentioned above, it has "four strategic priorities: Innovation, Inclusion, Regional Leadership and Internationalisation." Each of these, in turn, identifies priorities. The first priority under Innovation is to "Create new approaches to developing an open innovation culture, removing the barriers to innovative practice, and rewarding student and staff innovation". In total, Warwick has 16 such priorities, all of which are inspiring and clear signals of Warwick's chosen strategic direction. But are they priorities, in the sense defined above? They are more a commitment-to-prioritise than detailed priority-setting; this, however, is a deliberate intention to keep their strategy brief[90], with details being fleshed out elsewhere.

In Chapter 1, the section on How Strategy Works noted that university strategies do not need to specify details of their operational implementation "but strategy needs to be sufficiently clear about the choices it makes to give clear, unambiguous guidance to operational planners." Operational planners at Warwick have their work cut out to operationalise these strategic priorities. For example, some seem likely to be absolute commitments (e.g. equal opportunities for staff and students) whereas others may be discretionary and dependent on resource availability (e.g. grow intercultural interactions at Warwick).

Whilst the strategy at Warwick may require more operational work than if the strategic priorities had been clearer, some university strategies appear to make operational planning almost impossible. One strategy, for example has 41 "Key Priorities for the Next Year" and although these are numbered, it is unclear whether the numbers reflect priority. In one section, setting up a new internal management structure is the number one priority whereas committing to equality and inclusion is the sixth priority.

Key recommendations for 'priority' in university strategies:

1. Whilst priorities can be referred to within university strategies in various ways (e.g. conversationally or referring to the priorities of external organisations) there is one particular way of referring to priority in a strategy that needs to follow its own distinct set of rules. This is when a priority is 'set' for the organisation.
2. Priority-setting needs to be clearly identified as such within university strategies.
3. A set priority needs to be clear about what it refers to; what are the eligibility criteria that apply to this priority?
4. The priority-level should be clear. The highest priority – unqualified commitment –will be supported under all foreseeable circumstances. Below unqualified commitment, all priorities are relative. When resources are limited, priorities will only be supported if their relative priority is high enough.
5. Priorities may differ in how they need to be prioritised. Some may need the time and attention of people, others may need money and others may simply need a managerial decision. Where this is critical to their adoption, it may need to be referred to in the strategy.
6. Priorities may differ in why they have been prioritised. Some may be critical to the success of the entire strategy whilst others may be stand-alone initiatives upon which nothing else depends. Where this is critical to their adoption, it may need to be referred to in the strategy.
7. University strategies do not need to contain details of their operational implementation, but they do need to guide operational planners on the priorities upon which strategic success depends.

8 STRATEGY ELEMENT: PERFORMANCE

Data indicative of meaningful progress

Measures, targets and milestones, progress measures, key outcomes, key success measures, key achievement goals and markers of excellence: these are some of the ways the 52 university strategies analysed for this report say they will measure performance. The most commonly used terms for performance measures are 'Key Performance Indicators' and 'Targets' that, for this report, we define as follows:
1. Key Performance Indicators (KPIs) are dimension upon which success can be measured e.g. student satisfaction from the National Student Survey.
2. Targets are values used as a threshold to define success e.g. over 85% of students satisfied with the quality of their course in National Student Survey

Using these definitions, we found that the majority of strategies have KPIs and a minority have targets (Table 4).

Table 4 KPIs and Targets in university strategies (n=52)

	Yes	No
Do they have KPIs?	28 (54%)	24 (46%)
Do they have Targets?	14 (27%)	38 (73%)

To give an indication of some of the variation in performance measurement across university strategies, we have produced performance goal maps for 4 different universities (Figures 23 to 26).

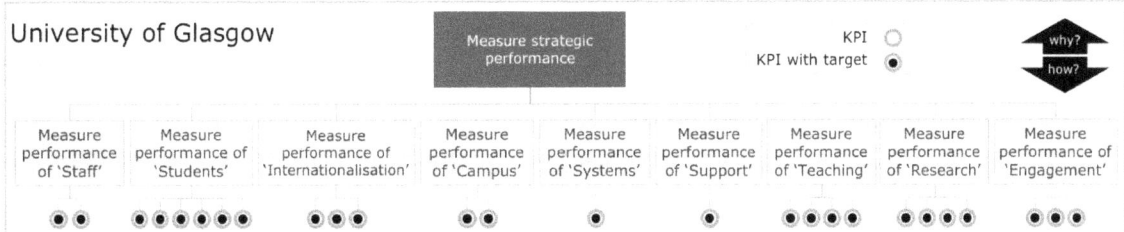

Figure 23 University of Glasgow performance goal map

University of Glasgow has 26 key performance indicators, all of which have targets.

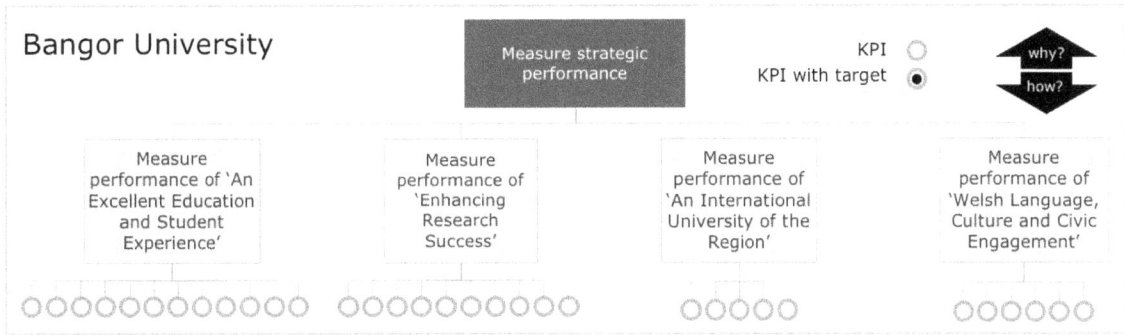

Figure 24 Bangor University performance goal map

Bangor University has 33 key performance indicators, none of which have targets.

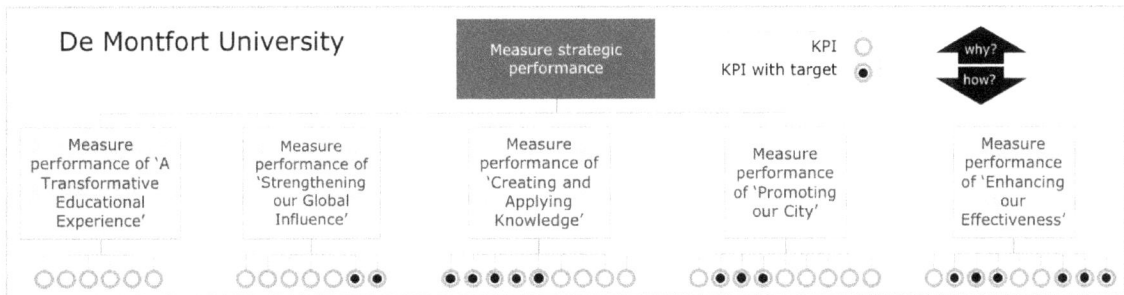

Figure 25 De Montfort performance goal map

De Montfort University has 40 key performance indicators, 16 of which have targets.

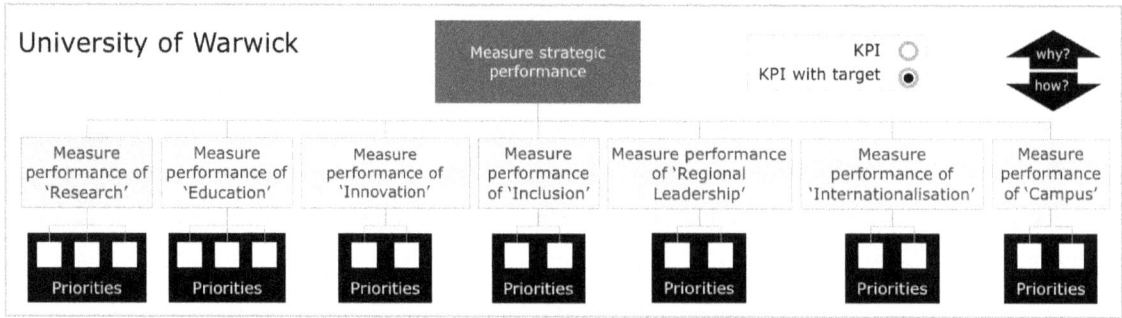

Figure 26 University of Warwick performance goal map

The **University of Warwick** has neither key performance indicators nor targets. Instead it identifies clear priorities within each section of its strategy (16 priorities in total) and these priorities are written in such a way as to be amenable to performance measurement. For example, one of the educational priorities is to "Ensure our students can progress into their choice of high quality employment through skills development, work experience, employer and alumni relations". This is readily measureable in terms of graduate employment and work experience and could, with some effort, be measureable in terms of skills progression and value-added from employers and alumni.

Key recommendations for 'performance' within university strategies:

Strategy is about change and, when change is mandated by strategy and invested-in during strategy deployment, good governance demands that the impact is measured. This, however, doesn't necessarily mean that every key performance indicator and target needs to be defined as part of strategy. Here, then, are our key recommendations for well-designed performance measurement in strategy.

1. Strategy needs to make a clear commitment to performance measurement. This should commit the university to measuring strategy performance across the lifetime of the strategy and clarify how this performance measurement will be governed and managed.
2. Strategy should map out the areas in which performance measurement should be undertaken to ensure that the measures employed are both sufficient and necessary to assess strategic impact.
3. During the strategy design process, the university should make clear and justified decisions on whether the strategy IS or IS NOT going to contain key performance indicators and targets, and follow through on that decision.
4. If the strategy does not contain key performance indicators and targets, the strategy should explain how KPIs will be decided and targets set.
5. A well-designed strategy will also define the performance management process for assessing strategic impact:
    a. How will the necessary data be collected, validated, aggregated, reconciled etc.?
    b. How will the data be analysed and progress assessed against targets?

      c. How will progress be reviewed and fed back into the overall strategy management process?
6. A well-designed strategy will also have performance-based contingency plans. How, for example will the strategy be reviewed and revised if performance greatly exceeds targets or fails to make significant progress towards targets?

9 STRATEGY ELEMENT: AGILITY

The ability and readiness to change

There is widespread recognition that the university sector is facing challenging times ahead. This was made explicit in many of the university strategy documents analysed for this report (Figure 27).

> "current challenging higher education environment"
> Aberystwyth University

> "rapidly changing political landscape"
> De Montford University

> "continued uncertainty in the external environment"
> Anglia Ruskin University

> "a profoundly challenging period for all UK universities" with "many current UK and global uncertainties."
> University of Sheffield

> "the education sector is responding to a very specific set of economic, social and political challenges. Over the next five years there will doubtless be further change and new and complex questions to grapple with."
> Brighton University

> "We live in a time of dramatic change, and the pace of that change is accelerating. This adds to the complexity and challenges already facing universities, but also presents many opportunities."
> University of Surrey

> "in ten years the world will be quite different from today"
> Imperial College London

> "Producing a long-term strategy during a period of unprecedented change, not only in our sector but politically, socially and economically, creates a challenge but many opportunities."
> University of Derby

> "the Higher Education environment is evolving rapidly and the pace of change will only get faster."
> The University of Nottingham

> "the environment for Higher Education is challenging"
> Bangor University

> "disruptive forces provide both risk and opportunity for traditional higher education"
> The University of Northampton

Figure 27 Challenges expressed in university strategies

So how should universities in general, and university strategies specifically, respond to such challenges? 11 of the 52 strategies analysed for this report highlighted the need for agility, across the entire organisation.

1. "Ours is a resilient and agile institution" "we will maintain a culture of flexibility and agility within the long-term pursuit of our goals." **University of Sheffield**. Sheffield then goes on to identify nine Guiding Principles, of which 'resilience' and 'agility' are two of them.
2. "Our strategy is ambitious. It focuses on growth and innovation, and calls on us to be agile and be prepared to take risks." **Bath Spa University**.
3. "This strategy is not meant to be static, but is instead an open and adaptive roadmap. Our ethos is one of pragmatism and agility, which will position us to take advantage of the new opportunities the future will bring." **University of Surrey**. The Surrey Strategy goes on to say "Our values underpin a strong culture of excellence, diversity, resilience and collaboration, which require us to be agile to change, and ready to adapt where and when we should."
4. "To be a successful university in the future, we will need to operate professionally with agility and pace" **Aston University**. Expanding on this, Aston goes on to say "to embed a high-performance culture across the organisation …[we must] operate energetically and dynamically, in a customer-focused manner, prioritising innovation and agility."
5. "A key determinant of a university's success will be not only how it adapts to, but how it embraces, change." **De Montfort University.**
6. "We will build a more agile, adaptive and resilient organisation so that we will be ready for whatever the future holds." And "as the frontiers of knowledge cannot be predicted, agility and flexibility are integral attributes for success." **Imperial College London**.
7. "Encourage streamlining of oversight and approval processes at all levels to increase our institutional agility." **University of Glasgow**.
8. "We have become an agile, effective and confident University … we will embrace transformational change and challenge enabled by our agile and effective management of both opportunities and risks." **Swansea University.**
9. "Our engaged, agile approach is attuned to the rapidly evolving global agenda." **Bath University**.
10. "We will empower our staff to operate effectively through a lean and agile approach to governance and management that enables staff to fulfil their roles and provides effective, transparent and accountable decision-making." **Bristol University**
11. "We are purposeful and agile in a changing world and work in innovative ways to achieve our goals." **Brunel University**. This is one of Brunel's values, labelled 'Determined'.

In addition, agility was also highlighted as being important for particular aspects of university work.
1. "Our strengths in research derive from: Our flexibility and agility which permit the formation of multi-disciplinary, international teams to respond to emerging opportunities and challenges." **University of Bath**
2. "We will adopt an agile approach in responding to the risks and opportunities associated with Brexit." **Queens University Belfast**
3. "A Digital Future … Digital techniques and technologies will … ensure that our University is renowned for being interactive, effective and agile." **University of Leicester**
4. "We will develop our working environment to ensure we are fleet of foot, agile and effective." **University of Lincoln**
5. "The University will actively manage both its income and expenditure in an agile and responsive manner which enables the University to react swiftly and effectively to any changes in the external funding environment." **University of Oxford**

So, the challenge of future uncertainties is felt widely and some universities commit themselves to agility in response. But what does agility mean? What provision needs to be made for agility to flourish? How would we evaluate whether our agility was of value to the organisation? Or even whether it was actually agile?

The word 'agile' comes from the Latin 'agere' and the suffix '-ile'. agere: act, do, move, perform, drive, urge or lead and -ile (suffix): pertaining to or having the characteristic of[91]. In common use it can apply to either movement or thought and it can refer to capability, readiness or action, as shown in Table 5.

Table 5 Definitions of 'agile'

	Movement	Thought
Capability	nimble; supple; lithe; dextrous; athletic	astute; quick-witted; clever; sharp
Readiness	active; lively; responsive	aware; perceptive; alert
Action	quick moving; vigorous; energetic; deft	quick thinking; prompt; rapid; decisive; effective

The concept of agility was first widely used in business by software engineers[92]. Before then, software was developed in what was called a waterfall process. Great efforts would be invested trying to specify everything the software needed to do prior to the start of development. Then software developers would produce all the specified features and launch the fully developed product in a single release. There were two problems with this approach.

Firstly, the business environment in which the software was to be used had often moved on between specification and release, making certain features obsolete before it was even used. Secondly, it is hard to specify the features of even moderately complex software prior to development. The need for features may only emerge as development progresses. Resolving one aspect of software design may change understanding of how best to define other aspects of the software. Solutions may be emergent during development. To try to resolve these problems, the agile movement was born. In 2001 a group of software engineers got together and wrote the Agile Manifesto[93], which can be summarised as follows:

1. The highest priority is to satisfy the customer;
2. Customer requirements change and these changes must be welcomed even late in development;
3. This is achieved by delivering working software frequently (from a couple of weeks to a couple of months);
4. Even more frequently, the software team and people from other parts of the business must work together closely to update and re-prioritise software requirements;
5. Working software is the primary measure of progress.

Applying the concept of agility to business in general (as opposed to software engineering), it is the ability of an organisation to sense and respond rapidly to market and environmental changes in productive and cost effective ways.[94] To be agile, an organisation needs to both think and work in agile ways.

To think in agile ways requires regularly refreshing knowledge of what is happening in the market and the wider environment that is important to the organisation. Then decisions about what the organisation focuses its efforts and resources on can be re-prioritised. This refresh and re-prioritising process needs to be strategic, customer-centric and evidence-based.

Working in agile ways requires vigilance in monitoring market and environmental conditions. It requires agile ways of working (or habits): working in sprints, producing minimum viable products, seeking continuous customer feedback, routine refinement and re-prioritisation of tasks. It requires innovation and, if innovation is to flourish it also requires agile governance. A goal map of business agility is shown in Figure 28.

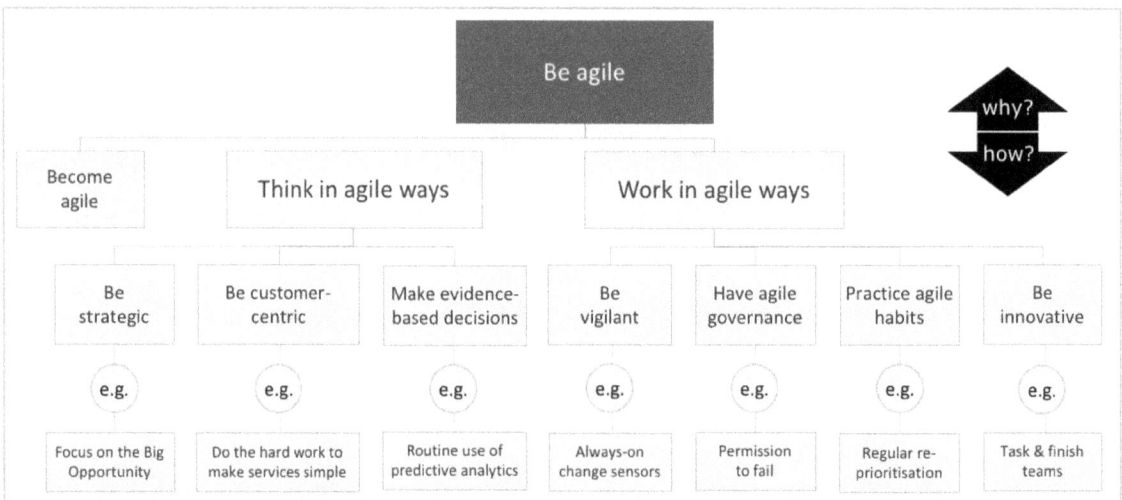

Figure 28 Goal map of business agility

How to be an agile university

Whilst, as we saw above, many universities commit themselves to agility, we have found only a few who spelled out, in their strategy documents <u>how</u> they intended to be agile.

University of Glasgow has a section in its strategy entitled "Implementation". It is introduced with this: "The ambitions of our strategy require a step change in our culture and the way we work. We have created three key work streams, each led by a member of senior management, and drawing on staff resources across the University." One of these workstreams is called "Agility" and is described as follows: "Research, innovation and enterprise are fast-moving fields of activity, and global tastes and trends in higher education can change overnight. We will streamline the way we work to ensure we are capable of keeping pace with the sea changes and emerging opportunities ahead."

The section of **Heriot-Watt University's** strategy called "Delivering our Strategy" is introduced as follows: "Our strategic plan has been informed by contributions from hundreds of our staff and students and it is presented as a living document. We live and work in an ever-changing environment, and the delivery of our strategy will be supported by continuous horizon scanning and monitoring of our performance."

The Vice-Chancellor's introduction to the **University of Nottingham's** strategy concludes by saying: "We will keep these goals and actions under constant review and make sure that we continue to respond to future challenges and competition, are dynamic and ambitious in our responses, and always try to act in the best long-term interests of our university."

University of Bath's strategy has eight core methods (which they call 'strategies') and one is titled "Develop the capability of our people to deliver our objectives and to respond flexibly to changing needs." It is described as follows: "Recruiting the best people and supporting them to realise their full potential will help us to deliver excellence. Investing in our leadership and management capacity will help us to support colleagues to respond flexibly to the changing needs of our students and other stakeholders."

And finally, as evidence of agility in action, **De Montfort University** introduced its strategy by saying "we are ready to renew and reframe the Strategic Plan, two years ahead of schedule."

Key recommendations for 'agility' within university strategies:

1. Make sure agility is included – how will strategy respond to the rapidly changing Higher Education environment without it?
2. Think carefully about which parts of your strategy need to be managed in an agile way. Not all will. Much of your strategy may be resilient to change; your values and vision, for example.
3. A good strategy will identify:
    a. what challenges and opportunities have been foreseen and taken into account in the strategy;
    b. what challenges and opportunities are foreseeable but have not been taken into account in the strategy;
    c. what monitoring will be done, and by whom, of changes to our marketplace and operating environment;
    d. how the strategy will be reviewed, by whom and when, if significant changes are foreseen;
    e. what capabilities we need to develop across the organisation to respond in an agile way to such changes;
    f. what resources we need to hold in reserve to support such changes;
    g. what governance we need in place to manage the organisation in an agile way;
    h. how we will measure whether our agile ways of thinking and working are performing satisfactorily.

10 STRATEGY ELEMENT: ADOPTION

Active engagement, willing commitment

A strategy can only drive change if it is adopted. Our analysis of university strategies has identified four ways to enable strategy adoption.

1. Consultation during strategy development

A great way to get buy-in to a strategy is to make people feel like they have been consulted and listened to as the strategy was being developed. This fosters a sense of community engagement and ownership of the strategy before it even exists. Several universities make reference to the consultation process that led to the strategy. The **University of Derby**, for example, says in its strategy that "in total, over 600 staff, around 100 students and over 20 stakeholders have contributed to the development of [this Strategic] Framework." The **University of Nottingham** says in its strategy that this "strategy framework is the product of extensive analysis and consultation with staff, students, alumni, partners and governors". The **University of Sheffield's** strategy says "The University Council and the University Executive Board have been thoroughly engaged in the process led by our Vice-Chancellor, Professor Sir Keith Burnett."

2. Strategy launch & communication

The launch of a new strategy provides a great opportunity to announce to the world what the university stands for and what impact it aspires to make. Several universities have taken the opportunity to announce this to the world as well as to staff and students. The **University of Bristol** launched its strategy at the Natural History Museum in London as well as a subsequent launch event in Bristol.[95] **Heriot-Watt University** held strategy launch events at each of its four campuses in Edinburgh, Scottish Borders, Orkney, Malaysia and Dubai.[96]

Communicating strategies, however, does not just have to be about holding launch events – utilising different channels and effectiveness of communication are key. Sull et al 2018 derived six steps to communicating strategic priorities effectively from their strategy research at MIT Sloan School of Management:[97]
1. Limit strategic priorities to a handful.
2. Provide a concise explanation of what a priority means
3. Clarify how a priority will be accomplished
4. Explain why a priority matters
5. Measure progress toward achieving the priority
6. Set specific targets for the future

Some universities have been innovative in how they communicate their new strategies. The **University of Northampton** had its Illustration students produce a graphical one-page strategy[98], which is supported by three accompanying documents that clarify what they mean by Super Supportive, Future Focused and Social Impact.

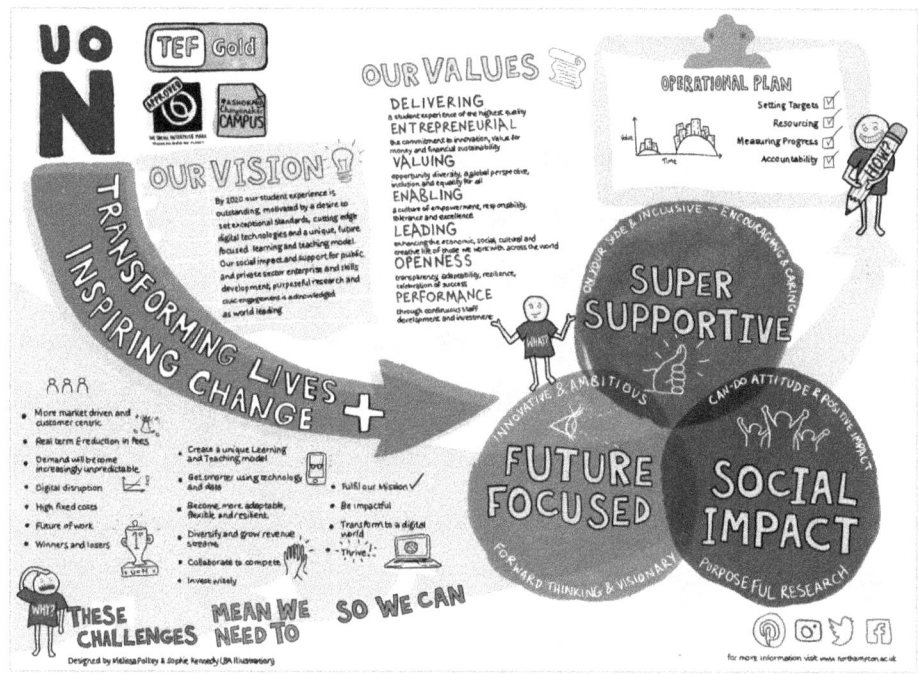

Figure 29 Single-page strategy produced by students from the University of Northampton

The **University of Dundee** has summarised its strategy in a 'Strategy Wheel' that is downloadable as a pdf[99] and the **University of the Arts, London** produced a short, leaflet-sized version of its strategy[100] as well as the full version[101].

3. Strategically-aligned resourcing

Implicit in many strategies is the notion that if you want resources flowing into your course, your department or your school, you need to stick to the strategy. What this notion lacks in subtlety it more than makes up for in effectiveness. **Anglia Ruskin University**'s strategy says "Underpinning this strategy will be an internally-facing three-year rolling operational plan. This will set out in greater detail the choices we need to make, the actions we will undertake to deliver on our strategic aims and a set of key performance indicators to help us measure our progress." **Kings College London**'s strategy says "we will prioritise activities that enable our financial sustainability so that we can invest in pursuits that may not generate revenue, but which will ensure the delivery of our Strategic Vision." **Aston University**'s strategy pledges to "invest in activities aligned to the strategy and end activities that are not." "Over time, we will reduce and cease activities not directly aligned with this strategy to make the best use of our resources and free up capacity to focus on areas of strength. We will conduct a review of research activities to reassign resources to research areas that align with our strategic strengths and industry relationships. We will also evaluate and, as necessary, restructure our educational offering to align with student outcomes ... This strategic plan will begin from spring 2018 with the development of a full five-year implementation plan to deliver the initiatives." **Brighton University** commits itself to "earmark a proportion of our budget each year for investment against explicit objectives set out in this strategy. We will work to maximise income and manage down our costs in order to achieve this."

4. Strategy governance and management

It is clearly important to ensure that senior managers and governors are fully committed to the strategy. This requires them to both support it and to avoid undermining it. The Chair of the University Council at the **University of Sheffield** said in his introduction to the university's strategy that "the themes presented in this Strategic Plan represent the areas requiring the University's focus over the next five years ... The University Council will monitor the University's progress against these high-level key ambitions on a regular basis." **Bangor University**'s strategy says that governance and management will "continually review the University's strategy to ensure that it remains fit for purpose and is responsive to the changing HE environment." In the interviews with senior university leaders for this research we were told of the agendas of both university governor meetings and the university senior management meeting being organised around the key themes or priorities in the university strategy. Another approach to securing effective management of strategic initiatives is to delegate ownership of them to individual senior managers. The **University of Salford's** strategy has a table showing its 14 Key Performance Indicators and which four are owned by the Deputy Vice Chancellor, which three are owned by each Pro Vice Chancellor, which two are owned by the Finance Director and which one is left for each of the Chief Operating Officer and the Director of Human Resources.

Strategy adoption, dealt with in detail

The majority of university strategies mention strategy adoption in a sentence or two. A few, however, go into detail about how they plan to ensure their strategy makes a difference. Here is a sample of three such universities.

The **University of Portsmouth**'s strategy says "Enabling the delivery of our vision [we will]:
1. fully align our academic and professional service staffing capacity and capabilities with our strategy, investing in development opportunities for all staff that enable them to contribute fully to delivery of our vision in appropriate ways …
2. recognise and reward staff contributions across our strategy and promote equality, diversity and wellbeing …
3. invest strategically in our IT, digital infrastructure and systems to ensure these support our ambitions effectively and efficiently."

The **University of Glasgow**'s strategy has an entire section on Implementation, which says: "The ambitions of our strategy require a step change in our culture and the way we work. We have created three key work streams, each led by a member of senior management, and drawing on staff resources across the University, to drive the strategic change necessary to secure our world-class status.
1. Empowering People: We want to be regarded among the very best higher education institutions in the world. For that to happen, all staff need to have a sense of ownership of their role and a responsibility for working towards the fulfilment of our strategic vision. We will create a culture of empowerment and provide tailored opportunities for staff at all levels to ensure that the University's success is driven by everyone.
2. Focus: We are proudly broad-based, and we have expertise in almost every field of human endeavour. Achieving world-class excellence requires us to be bolder about our strategic direction and commit greater investment in areas of research and teaching where we have the capability to lead the world. We will determine where these strengths lie and change the way we operate to align our resources with our strategy.
3. Agility: Research, innovation and enterprise are fast-moving fields of activity, and global tastes and trends in higher education can change overnight. We will streamline the way we work to ensure we are capable of keeping pace with the sea changes and emerging opportunities ahead."

The **University of Northampton** has a section in its strategy "Operations and Governance", which says:
1. "Single Business Plan. There is only one strategy – Transforming Lives + Inspiring Change. The risk of running a myriad of sub strategies is that they disrupt and divert the overall sense of strategic direction and add unnecessary complexity. Instead the unique interrelations and activities that underpin it are captured in a

single Business (operational) Plan. This is a fundamental document owned by the Senior Team that drives and executes our Mission and strategic response.
2. Balanced Scorecard (see also point 6 below). We will use the Balanced Scorecard method to translate strategy via each Critical Success Factor into a coherent and interrelated set of performance measures to guide the Business Plan for operations. The Balanced Scorecard captures a broad range of metrics that reflect our diverse activities and outputs and provides forward (lead) indicators in addition to more traditional financial and quality input data. The Balanced Scorecard for the University and its comprising elements and high level measures are shown as part of the strategy map. The high level measures will be reviewed annually by the Board and Senate and modified where appropriate.
3. Ownership and Accountability (see also point 6 below). Balanced Scorecard metrics will be cascaded through the organisation via the annual Staff Performance and Development Review (PDR). Maintaining clear line of sight between strategy and operations via the PDR is key to successful implementation. The Senior Team are responsible collectively and accountable collectively for a) managing the cascade process through the University and b) delivery against targets.
4. Risk and Opportunity Management. The broad assumptions and challenges faced by the University are set out in the introduction. Operational risk management is governed by the University's Senior Management Teams and monitored at Board level through monthly meetings. The Audit Committee and Project Assurance Committee, with support from internal and external auditors and sector-regulated bodies, provide additional assurance.
5. Role of the Board of Governors. The Board of Governors approves the strategic plan and direction of the University. They hold the executive to account in all matters relating to the good running of the University. The Board meets monthly. It will underpin the choices we make over the next period of our development."
6. In their revised Operational Plan 2018-2022, the Balanced Scorecard approach was replaced by a more dynamic approach to strategy management: Gap Analysis[102].

Key recommendations for 'adoption' within university strategies:

1. Be explicit about how the strategy is to be adopted, within the strategy itself.
2. Consider the four ways to encourage strategy adoption:
    a. Consultation during strategy development
    b. Strategy launch event
    c. Strategically-aligned resourcing
    d. Strategy governance and management.
3. The more difficult strategy adoption is expected to be, perhaps because of the magnitude of the changes or the anticipated resistance to those changes, the more detail needs to be included on strategy adoption.

11 UNIVERSITY STRATEGIES: THE FUTURE

The data in our sample suggests that 62.5% of university strategies currently have end dates in 2019, 2020 or 2021 and hence will need to be re-written and re-launched over the next few years.

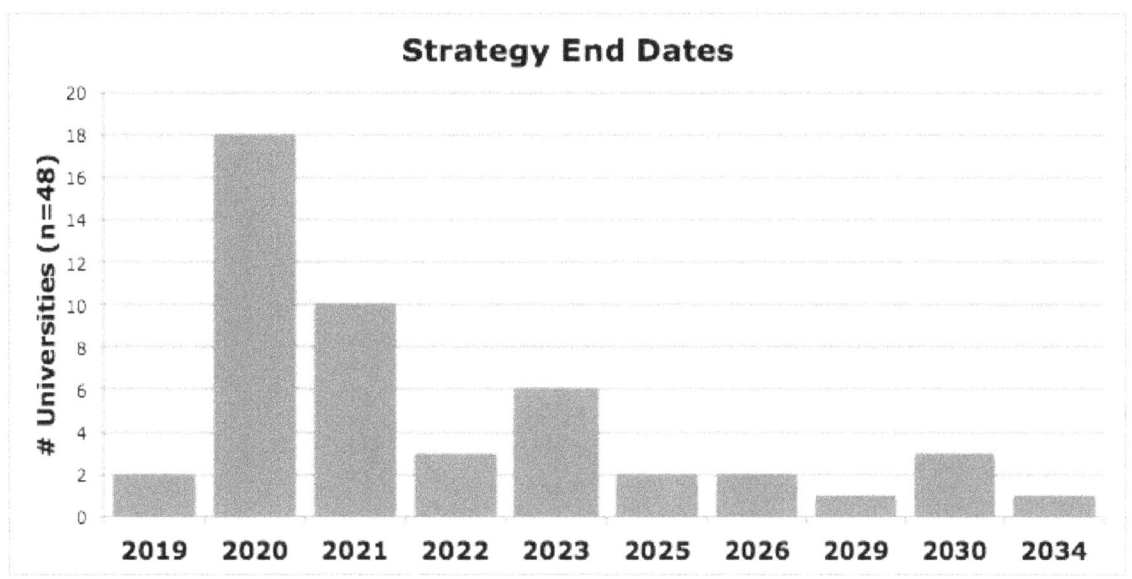

Figure 30 Strategy end dates

The sector also faces huge challenges; marketplace competition, changes in financial models and increasingly demanding 'customers'. This is, therefore, a critical time for strategic thinking in the university sector. So how should universities be preparing to write their strategies for the third decade of the third millennium? How can institutions develop the powerful, effective strategies required to respond to future challenges? What can we expect the future to hold? Based on the research done for this report, we propose below three drivers that will impact future university strategy development:

1 Strategy and strategic thinking will become much more important in the sector.
Whenever an organisation faces disruption, or even uncertainty, it becomes more important that budget is spent wisely and resources are deployed well. This requires careful analysis, clear decision-making and focused action. This is the stuff of strategy. In turbulent times, not only do universities need to be managed well, they also need to be seen to be managed well. This is another key role for strategy: providing a logical, consistent and coherent rationale for the decisions made and actions taken.

2 The time has come for strategy to start to have bite.
On the one hand Professor Sir Chris Husbands of **Sheffield Hallam University** says[103] "We are in a more financially exposed position than anyone in a leadership position has ever had to deal with … I expect the sector to look quite different in five year's time". On the other hand, Sir David Bell, Vice Chancellor of the **University of Sunderland**[104] is concerned that "for all the effort that went into seeking distinctiveness, [university] strategy documents ended up looking remarkably similar." University strategies, we believe, will become increasingly honest and transparent about the challenges they face and increasingly focused about how they intend to respond.

There are two other reasons we believe strategy will start to have more bite. The first is 'planning maturity'. Several of our interviewees for this report described how their university had undergone big changes in their planning capabilities over the past few years. Planning and resource allocation was a much more systematic and evidence-based annual process. Planning horizons had extended beyond a single year, often to five years in the future. The planning process was also better able to implement strategic priorities. This means that over the next few years, strategy and planning should become two sides of the same coin. Strategic priorities will need to drive planning priorities. Planners will need greater clarity from strategists about what their priorities actually mean. Planners will play a bigger role in sense-checking and validating strategic decisions. In short, planning maturity will demand greater strategic maturity. Or more bluntly, strategic immaturity will be increasingly exposed by planning maturity.

The second reason we believe strategy will start to have more bite is the 'professionalising of strategy' within universities. Strategy management has become a professional function within most universities, continuing a longer trend towards professionalising university management as a whole[105]. Strategic planners in UK universities now have their own professional membership organisation (HESPA – the Higher Education Strategic Planners Association). In his introduction to the book 'Higher Education Strategy and Planning: A Professional Guide'[106], Tony Strike declares his aim was 'to create a book that would be a showcase of the professional talent and techniques in strategic planning in higher education and provide a reflective critical evaluation of that practice.'

3 The time has come for strategy to start to have impact.
As we noted in Chapter 1 Richard Rumelt says there is inherent advantage in merely having a strategy. "The first natural advantage of good strategy arises because other organisations often don't have one … instead they have multiple goals and initiatives that symbolize progress, but no coherent approach to accomplish progress other than 'spend more and try harder'."[107] From this we would expect universities with well-designed strategies to thrive at the expense of those with poorer strategies or no strategy at all. UK Universities currently enjoy a world-leading status: we have roughly 1% of the world's population and somewhere between 11% and 40% of the world's top universities[108]. This will only continue if we decide how we seek to be world-leading and focus our efforts and resources at achieving it. Clearly, this is an internal management issue for universities but it is also a vital issue for the management of external relationships by universities. Since the decision by the Office for National Statistics at the end of 2018 to include a proportion of student loans as government expenditure[109], universities now need to make their case for public funding alongside the NHS, social care, schools and policing. From 2019 onwards, perhaps as never before, this needs to have a strategic clarity about the purpose of universities, the activities universities will focus their efforts on and the benefits this will bring to the country.

12 KEY RECOMMENDATIONS

Here are all the key recommendations from Chapters 3 to 10:

Strategy Element	Description	Summary of key recommendations
Destination	Where we are striving to get to	Define a coherent and meaningful purpose that is clear, focused, people-oriented and based on a need to change. Employ vision and values to provide stability and continuity across strategies.

Key recommendations for 'destination' within university strategies (Ch.3):

1. Strategies with a single, simple, clear 'destination' will be a lot more memorable than those with multiple complex goals.
2. Strategies with a single, tangible, specific 'destination' will be intrinsically more focused and will also enable more focused strategic decision-making. 'Which of these plausible alternatives will be more effective in getting us closer to our strategic destination?'
3. "Start with people!" This is Roger Martin and AG Lafley's advice for finding the high-order aspiration for an organisation.[110] What matters to our customers? What engages and motivates our staff (see 4 below)?
4. Good strategies give staff a coherent sense of purpose that engages and motivates them. Teresa Amabile's research[111] shows that a sense of tangible progress towards a meaningful purpose makes employees motivated and engaged at work more than pay, more than a good working relationship with their boss, more than praise and recognition.
5. Try to separate the destination of any particular strategy from the longer-term vision for the organisation. Vision and values are what should provide stability and continuity across strategies.
6. Remember that strategy destination is one part of the eight-piece jigsaw that makes up the Strategy Design Framework. A good destination is, therefore, one that will be reached by a small number of core methods working in concert. A good destination is one that aligns well with the obstacles and opportunities presented by the university's

operating environment AND aligns well with the evolving needs of university customers AND aligns well with the university's potential to transform. A good destination is one that supports innovation and forms part of a strategy that can be readily adopted by stakeholders.

Strategy Element	Description	Summary of key recommendations
Methods	Core activities to reach our destination	Identify a handful of pivotal core methods that are both sufficient and necessary to achieve strategic success (i.e. to get to the strategy destination).

Key recommendations for 'methods' within university strategies (Ch.4):

1. University strategies need to identify a handful of methods that together will be pivotal to achieving strategic success (to get to the strategy destination).
2. Methods need to be both sufficient and necessary to achieve the strategy destination.

Strategy Element	Description	Summary of key recommendations
Alignment	The logic connecting actions to outcomes	Ensure strategy is actionable across internal and external operating environments, and meets the need to change. Ensure internal consistency between strategies and sub-strategies.

Key recommendations for 'alignment' within university strategies (Ch.5):

1. Alignment is vital in strategy. It is what makes everyone pull in the same direction instead of pulling in different directions and making no impact.
2. There is a lot to align in a well-designed strategy: customers, competitors, suppliers as well as political and economic disruptors in the external operating environment; people, systems, ways-of-working, culture, values, governance and management in the internal environment.
3. Strategy also needs internal consistency and, where appropriate, consistency between any sub-strategies.
4. Goal mapping provides a rigorous, logical way to explore and validate the alignment of component parts of a strategy.

Strategy Element	Description	Summary of key recommendations
Innovation	The cultivation of new ways of thinking and working	Define innovation in terms of how it will drive change - what innovation is needed, why it is needed and how it will be both pursued and measured. Recognise and plan for resources, disruption and risks involved. Avoid 'fluff'.

Key recommendations for 'innovation' within university strategies (Ch.6):

1. Make sure innovation is included – how will strategy drive change without it?
2. Think carefully about how much innovation your strategy requires. The bolder and more

radical the strategy, the more innovation will be needed. The more innovation that is needed:
   a. the more resources will be needed to support it;
   b. the more disruptive it will be to the university's standard ways of working;
   c. the more risk there will be of innovation-failure, and possibly, as a result, of failure to meet strategic objectives.
3. Make sure innovation is defined in terms of:
   a. Why is innovation needed? How does it align with the rest of the strategy?
   b. What innovation is needed? Which aspect of the university needs to change and in what ways?
   c. How will the innovation be pursued? What initiatives or resources will support the innovation? How will we work differently to be innovative? Who is charged with leading the innovation?
   d. How will we know if the innovation has been successful? What success criteria or success metrics will be used to define success?
4. Make sure your strategy development process has a rigorous 'fluff-filter' around innovation.

Strategy Element	Description	Summary of key recommendations
Priority ★★☆	The identification of what really matters	Clearly identify, justify and set priority levels to ensure timely and effective allocation and deployment of resources.

Key recommendations for 'priority' in university strategies (Ch.7):

1. Whilst priorities can be referred to within university strategies in various ways (e.g. conversationally or referring to the priorities of external organisations) there is one particular way of referring to priority in a strategy that needs to follow its own distinct set of rules. This is when a priority is 'set' for the organisation.
2. Priority-setting needs to be clearly identified as such within university strategies.
3. A set priority needs to be clear about what it refers to; what are the eligibility criteria that apply to this priority?
4. The priority-level should be clear. The highest priority – unqualified commitment –will be supported under all foreseeable circumstances. Below unqualified commitment, all priorities are relative. When resources are limited, priorities will only be supported if their relative priority is high enough.
5. Priorities may differ in how they need to be prioritised. Some may need the time and attention of people, others may need money and others may simply need a managerial decision. Where this is critical to their adoption, it may need to be referred to in the strategy.
6. Priorities may differ in why they have been prioritised. Some may be critical to the success of the entire strategy whilst others may be stand-alone initiatives upon which

nothing else depends. Where this is critical to their adoption, it may need to be referred to in the strategy.
7. University strategies do not need to contain details of their operational implementation, but they do need to guide operational planners on the priorities upon which strategic success depends.

Strategy Element	Description	Summary of key recommendations
Performance ✓	Data indicative of meaningful progress	Commit to measuring performance to assess strategic impact, and define that performance measurement process. Ensure consistent use of measurement (e.g. KPIs and targets). Include performance-based contingency plans.

Key recommendations for 'performance' within university strategies (Ch.8):

Strategy is about change and, when change is mandated by strategy and invested-in during strategy deployment, good governance demands that the impact is measured. This, however, doesn't necessarily mean that every key performance indicator and target needs to be defined as part of strategy. Here, then, are our key recommendations for well-designed performance measurement in strategy.

1. Strategy needs to make a clear commitment to performance measurement. This should commit the university to measuring strategy performance across the lifetime of the strategy and clarify how this performance measurement will be governed and managed.
2. Strategy should map out the areas in which performance measurement should be undertaken to ensure that the measures employed are both sufficient and necessary to assess strategic impact.
3. During the strategy design process, the university should make clear and justified decisions on whether the strategy IS or IS NOT going to contain key performance indicators and targets, and follow through on that decision.
4. If the strategy does not contain key performance indicators and targets, the strategy should explain how KPIs will be decided and targets set.
5. A well designed strategy will also define the performance management process for assessing strategic impact:
    a. How will the necessary data be collected, validated, aggregated, reconciled etc.?
    b. How will the data be analysed and progress assessed against targets?
    c. How will progress be reviewed and fed back into the overall strategy management process?
6. A well-designed strategy will also have performance-based contingency plans. How, for example will the strategy be reviewed and revised if performance greatly exceeds targets or fails to make significant progress towards targets?

Strategy Element	Description	Summary of key recommendations
Agility	The ability and readiness to change	Ensure key parts of strategy are fit to respond swiftly and appropriately to foreseeable and unforeseeable challenges and opportunities. Be vigilant, then refresh and re-prioritise in a strategic, customer-centric and evidence-based way.

Key recommendations for 'agility' within university strategies (Ch.9):

1. Make sure agility is included – how will strategy respond to the rapidly changing Higher Education environment without it?
2. Think carefully about which parts of your strategy need to be managed in an agile way. Not all will. Much of your strategy may be resilient to change; your values and vision, for example.
3. A good strategy will identify:
    a. what challenges and opportunities have been foreseen and taken into account in the strategy;
    b. what challenges and opportunities are foreseeable but have not been taken into account in the strategy;
    c. what monitoring will be done, and by whom, of changes to our marketplace and operating environment;
    d. how the strategy will be reviewed, by whom and when, if significant changes are foreseen;
    e. what capabilities we need to develop across the organisation to respond in an agile way to such changes;
    f. what resources we need to hold in reserve to support such changes;
    g. what governance we need in place to manage the organisation in an agile way;
    h. how we will measure whether our agile ways of thinking and working are performing satisfactorily.

Strategy Element	Description	Summary of key recommendations
Adoption	Active engagement, willing commitment	Be explicit about how strategy is to be adopted. Consult during strategy development and promote strategy launch. Ensure strategically-aligned resourcing and rigorous strategy governance and management.

Key recommendations for 'adoption' within university strategies (Ch.10):

1. Be explicit about how the strategy is to be adopted, within the strategy itself.
2. Consider the four ways to encourage strategy adoption:
    a. Consultation during strategy development
    b. Strategy launch event
    c. Strategically-aligned resourcing
    d. Strategy governance and management.
3. The more difficult strategy adoption is expected to be, perhaps because of the magnitude of the changes or the anticipated resistance to those changes, the more detail needs to be included on strategy adoption.

APPENDIX 1 UNIVERSITIES SELECTED FOR THIS RESEARCH

The 52 universities included in the research for this report were selected using 4 criteria:
1. a selection of Russell Group and non-Russell Group universities;
2. high-ranking universities and those that had the biggest recent changes to their university rankings (up or down);
3. representations of universities from across the UK, including some that were in geographically similar locations (for comparison purposes)
4. a selection of small specialist universities.

University	Strategy Webpage	Strategy PDF download
Abertay University	https://www.abertay.ac.uk/about/the-university/governance-and-management/corporate-information/	https://www.abertay.ac.uk/media/2388/strategic_plan_2015_for_web.pdf
Aberystwyth University	https://www.aber.ac.uk/en/strategicplan/	https://www.aber.ac.uk/en/media/departmental/strategicplan/Strategic-Plan-individual-pages-pdf--En.pdf
Anglia Ruskin University	https://www.anglia.ac.uk/about-us/strategy-and-leadership	https://www.anglia.ac.uk/-/media/Files/corporate-documents/designing-our-future-2017-2026.pdf
Aston University	https://www2.aston.ac.uk/about/strategy/index	https://www2.aston.ac.uk/about/documents/Aston%20University%20Strategy%202018.pdf
Bangor University	https://www.bangor.ac.uk/planning-and-student-data/strategic-plan/index.php.en	https://www.bangor.ac.uk/planning-and-student-data/strategic-plan/strategic-plan-english-web.pdf
Bath Spa University	https://www.bathspa.ac.uk/about-us/vision-and-strategy/	*No PDF*
Brunel University London	https://www.brunel.ac.uk/about/brunel-2030	https://www.brunel.ac.uk/about/brunel-2030/docs/Brunel-Vision-2030.pdf
Canterbury Christ Church University	https://www.canterbury.ac.uk/about-us/strategic-framework-2015-2020.aspx	https://www.canterbury.ac.uk/about-us/docs/Strategic-Framework-2015-2020.pdf
Cardiff University	http://www.cardiff.ac.uk/thewayforward	http://www.cardiff.ac.uk/__data/assets/pdf_file/0015/10347/TheWayForward2018EngWeb.pdf

Coventry University	https://www.coventry.ac.uk/the-university/about-coventry-university/our-corporate-plan/	https://www.coventry.ac.uk/globalassets/media/global/09-about-us/who-we-are/corporate-strategy-2021.pdf
De Montfort University	https://www.dmu.ac.uk/about-dmu/university-governance/strategic-plan/index.aspx	https://www.dmu.ac.uk/documents/university-governance/strategic-plan-2018-23.pdf
Heriot-Watt University	https://strategy2025.hw.ac.uk/	*No PDF*
Imperial College London	https://www.imperial.ac.uk/strategy/	https://www.imperial.ac.uk/media/imperial-college/about/leadership-and-strategy/public/Strategy2015-2020.pdf
King's College London	https://www.kcl.ac.uk/aboutkings/strategy	http://www.kcl.ac.uk/aboutkings/strategy/Kings-strategic-vision-2029.pdf
Kingston University	https://www.kingston.ac.uk/aboutkingstonuniversity/howtheuniversityworks/universityplan/	https://www.kingston.ac.uk/documents/aboutkingstonuniversity/howtheuniversityworks/universityplan/documents/Corporate_Plan.pdf
Loughborough University	https://www.lboro.ac.uk/strategy/	*No PDF*
Manchester Metropolitan University	https://www2.mmu.ac.uk/about-us/strategy/	https://www2.mmu.ac.uk/media/mmuacuk/content/documents/about/corporate-strategy/Manchester-Met-Corporate-Brochure-A6.pdf
Oxford Brookes University	https://www.brookes.ac.uk/about-brookes/strategy/strategy-2020/	*No PDF*
Queen's University Belfast	https://www.qub.ac.uk/corporate-plan/	www.qub.ac.uk/home/corporate-plan/Filestore/Filetoupload,749596,en.pdf
Robert Gordon University	https://www.rgu.ac.uk/rgustrategy	https://www.rgu.ac.uk/files/112/All-Files/201/RGU-Strategy-Map.pdf
Royal Academy of Music	https://www.ram.ac.uk/about-us/about-the-academy/management/strategies	https://www.ram.ac.uk/public/uploads/documents/0d280f_strategic-plan-2014-19.pdf

Solent University	https://www.solent.ac.uk/about/mission-and-strategy	https://www.solent.ac.uk/about/documents/southampton-solent-university-strategy-2015-2020.pdf
Staffordshire University	http://www.staffs.ac.uk/about/strategic-plan	http://www.staffs.ac.uk/about/pdf/connected-university-strategy.pdf
Swansea University	*No current webpage*	https://www.swansea.ac.uk/media/strategic-plan-2020-english.pdf
The London School of Economics and Political Science	http://www.lse.ac.uk/about-lse/our-strategy	https://info.lse.ac.uk/staff/services/Policies-and-procedures/Assets/Documents/strLsePla.pdf
University College London	https://www.ucl.ac.uk/2034/	*No PDF*
University of Aberdeen	https://www.abdn.ac.uk/about/strategy-and-governance/strategic-plan-20152020-735.php	https://www.abdn.ac.uk/about/documents/Strategic_Plan.pdf
University of Bath	https://www.bath.ac.uk/corporate-information/university-strategy-2016-to-2021/	https://www.bath.ac.uk/publications/university-of-bath-strategy-2016-to-2021/attachments/university-of-bath-strategy-2016-2021.pdf
University of Brighton	https://www.brighton.ac.uk/practical-wisdom/index.aspx	https://staff.brighton.ac.uk/mac/public_docs/strategy/University-Strategy-2016-2021.pdf
University of Bristol	http://www.bristol.ac.uk/university/strategy/	http://www.bristol.ac.uk/media-library/sites/university/documents/governance/policies/university-strategy.pdf
University of Cambridge	https://www.cam.ac.uk/about-the-university/how-the-university-and-colleges-work/the-universitys-mission-and-core-values	*No PDF*
University of Chester	https://www1.chester.ac.uk/about/the-university/corporate-plan-vision-2020	http://www.chester.ac.uk/sites/files/chester/Corporate_Plan_2015.pdf
University of Derby	https://www.derby.ac.uk/about/strategic-framework/	https://www.derby.ac.uk/media/derbyacuk/assets/organisation/about-us/Strategic-Framework-Brochure.pdf

University of Dundee	https://www.dundee.ac.uk/strategy/	*No PDF*
University of Essex	https://www.essex.ac.uk/about/strategic-plan	https://www.essex.ac.uk/-/media/documents/about/strategic-plan.pdf
University of Exeter	http://www.exeter.ac.uk/ourstrategy/	http://www.exeter.ac.uk/media/universityofexeter/corporatestrategy/Our_Strategy_2016_to_2021.pdf
University of Glasgow	https://www.gla.ac.uk/explore/strategy/	https://www.gla.ac.uk/media/media_410447_en.pdf
University of Leeds	http://hr.leeds.ac.uk/info/60/strategy_values_and_standards/229/the_university_strategy_values_and_standards	http://www.leeds.ac.uk/download/76/strategic_plan_2015
University of Leicester	https://le.ac.uk/about/strategy-development/strategy	https://le.ac.uk/~/media/uol/docs/publications/strategic-plan-sign-off-print.pdf
University of Lincoln	https://www.lincoln.ac.uk/home/abouttheuniversity/managementandstrategy/	https://www.lincoln.ac.uk/home/media/responsive2017/abouttheuniversity/managementandstrategy/UOL,Strategic,Plan,(MAR,2016),V5Final.pdf
University of Liverpool	https://www.liverpool.ac.uk/strategy-2026/	http://www.liverpool.ac.uk/strategy-2026/documents/OurStrategy2026.pdf
University of Northampton	https://www.northampton.ac.uk/more/governance-and-management/office-of-the-vice-chancellor/transforming-lives-inspiring-change/	https://www.northampton.ac.uk/wp-content/uploads/2015/10/Strategic-plan-2018.pdf
University of Nottingham	https://www.nottingham.ac.uk/about/global-strategy-2020/index.aspx	https://www.nottingham.ac.uk/about/documents/uon-global-strategy-2020.pdf
University of Oxford	http://www.ox.ac.uk/about/organisation/strategic-plan-2018-23	http://www.ox.ac.uk/sites/files/oxford/field/field_document/Strategic%20Plan%202018-23.pdf
University of Portsmouth	https://www.port.ac.uk/about-us/our-strategy	https://www.port.ac.uk/-/media/files/about-us/our-strategy/full-design-pdfs/university-strategy.ashx

University of Salford	http://www.salford.ac.uk/about-us/corporate-information/strategy	http://www.salford.ac.uk/__data/assets/pdf_file/0006/817548/University-Strategy-2016-21.pdf
University of Sheffield	http://ourplan.group.shef.ac.uk/ourplan/	http://ourplan.group.shef.ac.uk/ourplan/wp-content/uploads/2015/12/TUOS-Strategic-Plan.pdf
University of Surrey	https://www.surrey.ac.uk/about/strategy/corporate-strategy-2017-22	https://www.surrey.ac.uk/sites/default/files/corporate-strategy-2017-2022.pdf
University of Sussex	https://www.sussex.ac.uk/strategy/	*No PDF*
University of the Arts London	https://www.arts.ac.uk/about-ual/strategy-and-governance/strategy	https://www.arts.ac.uk/__data/assets/pdf_file/0022/12838/UAL-Strategy-2015-22.pdf
University of Warwick	https://warwick.ac.uk/about/strategy/	https://warwick.ac.uk/about/strategy/6137_uow_university_strategy_landscape_v29_hr.pdf
University of York	https://www.york.ac.uk/about/mission-strategies/	https://www.york.ac.uk/media/abouttheuniversity/governanceandmanagement/documents/University-Strategy-2014-2020-revised-June-2016.pdf

REFERENCES

[1] "A quarter of total income received by UK universities in 2015–16 came from government sources, compared with a figure of around 45% for income from government sources in 2006–07." Universities UK Patterns and trends in UK Higher Education 2017. https://www.universitiesuk.ac.uk/facts-and-stats/data-and-analysis/Documents/patterns-and-trends-2017.pdf p40

[2] The Economist 2017 Growing competition between universities is changing student life. https://www.economist.com/britain/2017/02/23/growing-competition-between-universities-is-changing-student-life

[3] Chadwick S and Kew-Fickus O 2018. The planning cycle: a strategic conversation. Chapter 4 in Strike T (ed) Higher Education Strategy and Planning. Routledge, London.

[4] Robertson SL and Olds K 2018 Locating universities in a globalizing world. Chapter 1 in Strike T (ed) Higher Education Strategy and Planning. Routledge, London. p 14

[5] Moran H and Powell J 2018 Running a tight ship: can universities plot a course through rough seas? Research report by Shift Learning for the Guardian, supported by HSBC and in partnership with UUK. https://uploads.guim.co.uk/2018/01/30/Guardian_HSBC_UUK_Research_full_report_V4.pdf p 6.

[6] Sir David Bell's introduction to PA Consulting's Protected Past, Precarious Future: Tenth survey of heads of UK higher education institutions. https://www.paconsulting.com/insights/2019/our-tenth-university-vice-chancellor-survey/

[7] https://www.merriam-webster.com/dictionary/mission

[8] https://en.oxforddictionaries.com/definition/mission

[9] http://www.businessdictionary.com/definition/mission-statement.html

[10] https://www.thebalancesmb.com/mission-statement-2947996

[11] https://en.wikipedia.org/wiki/Mission_statement

[12] https://www.merriam-webster.com/dictionary/vision

[13] https://en.oxforddictionaries.com/definition/vision

[14] https://seapointcenter.com/what-is-vision/

[15] https://corporatefinanceinstitute.com/resources/knowledge/strategy/vision-statement/

[16] Cascade. How to write a good vision statement. https://www.executestrategy.net/blog/write-good-vision-statement/

[17] https://www.themarketingblender.com/vision-mission-statements/

[18] Change Factory. The components of a good vision statement. https://www.changefactory.com.au/our-thinking/articles/the-components-of-a-good-vision-statement/

[19] Oxford English Dictionary https://en.oxforddictionaries.com/definition/strategy

[20] Rumelt R 2011. Good Strategy Bad Strategy: The Difference and Why it Matters. Profile Books, NY. p 51

[21] https://en.oxforddictionaries.com/definition/value

[22] https://www.collinsdictionary.com/dictionary/english/values

[23] https://www.ethics.org/resources/free-toolkit/definition-values/

[24] http://www.businessdictionary.com/definition/values.html

[25] Rumelt R 2011. Good Strategy Bad Strategy: The Difference and Why it Matters. Profile Books, NY. p 4

[26] Rumelt R 2011. Good Strategy Bad Strategy: The Difference and Why it Matters. Profile Books, NY. p 7

[27] The Baldrige Glossary http://www.baldrige21.com/BALDRIGE_GLOSSARY/BN/Strategic_Challenges.html

[28] Bennett N and Lemoine GJ 2014. What VUCA really means for you. Harvard Business Review Jan-Feb 2014 issue. https://hbr.org/2014/01/what-vuca-really-means-for-you

[29] Roxburgh C 2009. The Use and Abuse of Scenarios. McKinsey Strategy & Corporate

Finance, November 2009. https://www.mckinsey.com/business-functions/strategy-and-corporate-finance/our-insights/the-use-and-abuse-of-scenarios

[30] Porter ME 1996. What is Strategy? Harvard Business Review 31st October 1996

[31] Rumelt R 2011. Good Strategy Bad Strategy: The Difference and Why it Matters. Profile Books, NY. p 79

[32] Lafley AG 2013 Strategy as Winning. In Lafley AG and Martin RL 2013 Playing to Win: How Strategy Really Works. Harvard Business Review Press, Boston p 48

[33] Rumelt R 2011. Good Strategy Bad Strategy: The Difference and Why it Matters. Profile Books, NY. p 84

[34] The Thinkers50 Ranking 2017 Rank #1 Roger Martin. https://thinkers50.com/t50-ranking/

[35] Martin RL 2013. Don't Let Strategy Become Planning. Harvard Business Review. 5th February 2013. https://hbr.org/2013/02/dont-let-strategy-become-plann

[36] Rumelt R 2011. Good Strategy Bad Strategy: The Difference and Why it Matters. Profile Books, NY. p 6

[37] Rumelt R 2011. Good Strategy Bad Strategy: The Difference and Why it Matters. Profile Books, NY. p 87

[38] Sull D, Homkes R and Sull C 2015. Why Strategy Execution Unravels—and What to Do About It. Harvard Business Review March 2015 issue. https://hbr.org/2015/03/why-strategy-execution-unravelsand-what-to-do-about-it

[39] https://en.oxforddictionaries.com/definition/strategy

[40] Rumelt R 2011. Good Strategy Bad Strategy: The Difference and Why it Matters. Profile Books, NY. p 11

[41] Denning S 2014. The Best of Peter Drucker. Forbes Magazine. 29th July 2014. https://www.forbes.com/sites/stevedenning/2014/07/29/the-best-of-peter-drucker/#3dcad5c05a96

[42] Drucker P 2011 Management. Abridged and revised edition of the original 1974

Management: Tasks, Responsibilities, Practices. Routledge, NY. p114

[43] "What gets measured gets managed" is frequently attributed to Peter Drucker but, in fact probably originates in the thinking of Lord Kelvin – see https://athinkingperson.com/2012/12/02/who-said-what-gets-measured-gets-managed/

[44] McGrath RG 2013 The End of Competitive Advantage: How to Keep Your Strategy Moving as Fast as Your Business. Harvard Business Review Press, Boston.

[45] Kinni T 2014. Rita Gunther McGrath on the End of Competitive Advantage. Strategy + Business Spring 2014, Issue 74. https://www.strategy-business.com/article/00239?gko=ede47

[46] McGrath RG https://www.ritamcgrath.com/books/the-end-of-competitive-advantage/

[47] Tabrizi B 2014. The Key to Change is Middle Management. Harvard Business Review 27th October 2014. https://hbr.org/2014/10/the-key-to-change-is-middle-management

[48] https://issuu.com/ As an example of a University strategy on Issuu see the University of Derby strategy at https://issuu.com/university_of_derby/docs/strategic_framework_2018-2030__univ

[49] https://www.yudu.com/   As an example of a University strategy on Yudu see the University of Aberdeen at http://content.yudu.com/htmlReader/A3xceo/UoA-Strategic-Plan/reader.html

[50] https://seapointcenter.com/what-is-vision/

[51] https://corporatefinanceinstitute.com/resources/knowledge/strategy/vision-statement/

[52] Cascade. How to write a good vision statement. https://www.executestrategy.net/blog/write-good-vision-statement/

[53] https://www.themarketingblender.com/vision-mission-statements/

[54] Change Factory. The components of a good vision statement. https://www.changefactory.com.au/our-thinking/articles/the-components-of-a-good-vision-statement/

[55] http://www.businessdictionary.com/definition/mission-statement.html

[56] https://www.thebalancesmb.com/mission-statement-2947996

[57] https://en.wikipedia.org/wiki/Mission_statement

[58] Bresciani A 2015. 51 Mission Statement Examples from The World's Best Companies. https://www.alessiobresciani.com/foresight-strategy/51-mission-statement-examples-from-the-worlds-best-companies/

[59] https://www.ethics.org/resources/free-toolkit/definition-values/

[60] http://www.businessdictionary.com/definition/values.html

[61] https://tagcrowd.com/

[62] Martin RL 2013. Don't Let Strategy Become Planning. Harvard Business Review. 5th February 2013. https://hbr.org/2013/02/dont-let-strategy-become-plann

[63] Rumelt R 2011. Good Strategy Bad Strategy: The Difference and Why it Matters. Profile Books, NY. p 11

[64] Lafley AG and Martin RL 2013 Playing to Win: How Strategy Really Works. Harvard Business Review Press, Boston p 35

[65] Teresa Amabile and Steven Kramer 2011. The Progress Principle. Harvard Business Review Press

[66] Sull D, Turconi S, Sull C and Yoder J 2018. Turning Strategy Into Results. MIT Sloan Management Review Spring 2018. https://sloanreview.mit.edu/article/turning-strategy-into-results/

[67] Rumelt R 2011. Good Strategy Bad Strategy: The Difference and Why it Matters. Profile Books, NY. p 6

[68] Rumelt R 2011. Good Strategy Bad Strategy: The Difference and Why it Matters. Profile Books, NY. p 77

[69] Sull D and Eisenhartd KM 2015 Simple Rules: How to Thrive in a Complex World. Houghton Mifflin Harcourt, NY. p 7

[70] Rumelt R. Good Strategy/Bad Strategy: The Difference and Why it Matters. Profile

Books, NY. p. 4

[71] Matthews E 2018 University launched new five-year strategic plan for 2018-2023. The Saint Newspaper, 8th November 2018. http://www.thesaint-online.com/2018/11/university-launches-new-five-year-strategic-plan-for-2018-2023/

[72] https://www.gov.uk/government/news/prime-minister-launches-major-review-of-post-18-education

[73] The VW famework was developed (by Goal Atlas) during the research for this report. It is however, an extension of the 'W-model' from Kachaner N, King K and Stewart S 2016 Four Best Practices for Strategic Planning. Boston Consulting Group. https://www.bcg.com/en-gb/publications/2016/growth-four-best-practices-strategic-planning.aspx (Full disclosure: Mike's wife Cathy has been the proud driver of a classic VW camper van for many years, so we are all big VW fans!)

[74] Donaldson G 1995. A New Tool for Boards: The Strategic Audit. Harvard Business Review, July/August 1995 Issue. https://hbr.org/1995/07/a-new-tool-for-boards-the-strategic-audit

[75] University of Dundee 2017 University Strategy https://www.dundee.ac.uk/strategy/

[76] University of Dundee 2008 Estates Strategy https://www.dundee.ac.uk/media/dundeewebsite/qualityframework/documents/Retention%20and%20progression%20strategy%202014.pdf

[77] University of Dundee 2018 Retention and Progression Strategy https://www.dundee.ac.uk/media/dundeewebsite/qualityframework/documents/Retention%20and%20progression%20strategy%202014.pdf

[78] University of York University Strategy 2014-2020. https://www.york.ac.uk/about/mission-strategies/universitystrategy2014-2020/

[79] University of York, Supporting Strategies. https://www.york.ac.uk/about/mission-strategies/universitystrategy2014-2020/

[80] Lafley AG and Martin RL 2013 Playing to Win: How Strategy Really Works. Harvard Business Review Press, Boston p 15-16

[81] Rumelt R. Good Strategy/Bad Strategy: The Difference and Why it Matters. Profile Books, NY. p. 85

[82] The Lawrence D Miles Value Engineering Reference Centre Collection at the University of Wisconsin-Madison. https://minds.wisconsin.edu/handle/1793/301

[83] Miles LD 2015. Techniques of Value Analysis and Value Engineering, 3rd Edition. Lawrence D Miles Value Foundation.

[84] https://en.wikipedia.org/wiki/Lawrence_D._Miles

[85] Bytheway CW 2007 FAST Creativity and Innovation. J Ross Publishing, Fort Lauderdale, Florida.

[86] Baxter MR 1995 Product Design: Practical methods for the systematic development of new products. Routledge, London p. 238

[87] Rumelt R. Good Strategy/Bad Strategy: The Difference and Why it Matters. Profile Books, NY. p. 37

[88] Tinworth A 2017 The lesson of the Museum of Failure is that innovation means risk. https://nextconf.eu/2017/06/lesson-museum-failure-innovation-means-risk/

[89] https://www.greenes.org.uk/greenes-education/our-history/the-history-of-the-tutorial/

[90] Feedback on draft report from Dr Richard Hutchins, Director of Strategy, University of Warwick, 21st March 2019.

[91] Barnhart RK (ed) 1988 Chambers Dictionary of Etymology. Chambers, Edinburgh.

[92] For a quick introduction to how agile applies to software development, see Blossom's three part-series of articles: https://www.blossom.co/blog/agile-software-history https://www.blossom.co/blog/what-is-agile-part-2 and https://www.blossom.co/blog/agile-product-market-fit

[93] See the Agile Manifesto itself at https://agilemanifesto.org/ and the principles behind it at https://agilemanifesto.org/principles.html

[94] Adapted from https://en.wikipedia.org/wiki/Business_agility (accessed 2nd March 2019)

[95] University of Bristol Press Release 2016 Plans for a second city campus unveiled in University of Bristol's new strategy. http://www.bristol.ac.uk/news/2016/november/new-strategy.html

[96] Heriot-Watt University News 2019 Upcoming Strategy 2025 launch events at Heriot-Watt campuses. https://www.hw.ac.uk/about/news/internal/2019/reminder-strategy-2025-launch-events-at-all.htm

[97] Sull D, Turconi S and Sull C 2018. Six Steps to Communicating Strategic Priorities Effectively. MIT Sloan Management Review 19th January 2018. https://sloanreview.mit.edu/article/six-steps-to-communicating-strategic-priorities-effectively/

[98] One page summary of the University of Northampton strategy by Sophie Kennedy and Melissa Polkey (BA Illustration) https://www.northampton.ac.uk/wp-content/uploads/2015/10/Transforming-Lives-and-Inspiring-Change-Our-Vision-hand-drawn.pdf

[99] University of Dundee Strategy Wheel Download. https://www.dundee.ac.uk/media/dundeewebsite/strategy/images/strategy-wheel-full.png

[100] https://www.arts.ac.uk/__data/assets/pdf_file/0023/12839/UAL-Strategy-2015-22-Summary-Spreads.pdf

[101] https://www.arts.ac.uk/__data/assets/pdf_file/0022/12838/UAL-Strategy-2015-22.pdf

[102] Personal communication with Professor Nick Petford, Vice-Chancellor, University of Northampton 26th March 2019

[103] Professor Sir Chris Husbands, quoted in Branwen Jeffrey's The University Time Bomb, BBC Radio 4 https://www.bbc.co.uk/programmes/m0003z38

[104] Sir David Bell's introduction to PA Consulting's Protected Past, Precarious Future: Tenth survey of heads of UK higher education institutions. https://www.paconsulting.com/insights/2019/our-tenth-university-vice-chancellor-survey/

[105] There is a significant academic literature on the professionalising of university management, including Deem, R 1998. 'New managerialism' and higher education: The management of performances and cultures in universities in the United Kingdom.

International Studies in Sociology of Education 8: 47-70. Middlehurst R 2013. Changing Internal Governance: Are Leadership Roles and Management Structures in United Kingdom Universities Fit for the Future? Higher Education Quarterly 67 (3): 275–294. Shepherd S 2016. No room at the top? The glass wall for professional services managers in pre-1992 English universities. Perspectives: Policy and Practice in Higher Education 21: 129-134.

[106] Strike T (ed) 2018 Higher Education Strategy and Planning: A Professional Guide Routledge, London.

[107] Rumelt R 2011. Good Strategy Bad Strategy: The Difference and Why it Matters. Profile Books, NY. p 11

[108] The QS World University Rankings feature 4 UK universities in their 2019 top 10, giving us 40% of the world's top Universities (https://www.topuniversities.com/university-rankings/world-university-rankings/2019). By contrast the THE World University Rankings have 11 UK universities in their top 100, suggesting we have 11% of the world's top universities (https://www.timeshighereducation.com/world-university-rankings/2019/world-ranking).

[109] Office for National Statistics 2018 New treatment of student loans in the public sector finances and national accounts. https://www.ons.gov.uk/economy/governmentpublicsectorandtaxes/publicsectorfinance/articles/newtreatmentofstudentloansinthepublicsectorfinancesandnationalaccounts/2018-12-17

[110] Lafley AG and Martin RL 2013 Playing to Win: How Strategy Really Works. Harvard Business Review Press, Boston p 35

[111] Teresa Amabile and Steven Kramer 2011. The Progress Principle. Harvard Business Review Press

www.ingramcontent.com/pod-product-compliance
Lightning Source LLC
Chambersburg PA
CBHW051317110526
44590CB00031B/4383